GUINNESS WORLD RECORDS Super Sports

by Shirley Pearson and Kathy Furgang

Carson-Dellosa Publishing LLC
Greensboro, North Carolina

GUINNESS WORLD RECORDS DISCLAIMER: Guinness World Records Limited has a very thorough accreditation system for records verification. However, while every effort is made to ensure accuracy, Guinness World Records Limited cannot be held responsible for any errors contained in this work. Feedback from our readers on any point of accuracy is always welcome.

SAFETY DISCLAIMER: Attempting to break records or set new records can be dangerous. Appropriate advice should be taken first, and all record attempts are undertaken entirely at the participant's risk. In no circumstances will Guinness World Records Limited or Carson-Dellosa Publishing LLC have any liability for death or injury suffered in any record attempts. Guinness World Records Limited has complete discretion over whether to include any particular records in the annual Guinness World Records book.

Due to the publication date, the facts and the figures contained in this book are current as of January 2011.

© 2012 Guinness World Records Limited

Visit Guinness World Records at *www.guinnessworldrecords.com*.

Credits

Content Editor: Christine Schwab

Copy Editor: Julie B. Killian

Layout and Cover Design: Van Harris

Carson-Dellosa Publishing LLC
PO Box 35665
Greensboro, NC 27425 USA
www.carsondellosa.com

ISBN 978-1-60996-466-5

01-335111151

TABLE OF CONTENTS

SETTING GUINNESS WORLD RECORDS RECORDS

Guinness World Records accomplishments are facts or events that belong in one of eight categories:

- Human Body
- Amazing Feats
- Natural World
- Science and Technology
- Arts and Media
- Modern Technology
- Travel and Transport
- Sports and Games

Some records are new because they are exciting and involve events that have never been attempted before. People with unique talents or features are also permitted to become record setters. However, many of the records are already established, and people try to find records that they can break. One record holder, Ashrita Furman, has broken or set more than 300 records since 1979.

Guinness World Records receives more than 60,000 requests each year. Record setters and breakers must apply first so that their attempts are official. The organization sets guidelines for each event to make sure that it can be properly measured. Guinness World Records also makes sure that all record breakers follow the same steps so that each participant gets an equal chance. Professional judges make sure that the guidelines are followed correctly and measured accurately. However, the guidelines may designate other community members who can serve as judges to witness an event. Once the record attempt is approved, the participant gets a framed certificate. The person's name may also be included in the yearly publication or on the Guinness World Records Web site at *www.guinnessworldrecords.com*.

BE A RECORD BREAKER!

Hey, kids!

Tubby is a Labrador retriever that collected and recycled about 26,000 plastic bottles from his daily walks. Rob Williams (USA) made a sandwich with his feet in less than two minutes. Tiana Walton (UK) placed 27 gloves on one hand at one time. Aaron Fotheringham (USA) landed the first wheelchair backflip. The Heaviest Pumpkin ever weighed 1,725 pounds (782.45 kg). And Rosi, the Heaviest Spider ever, is larger than a dinner plate. What do all of these stories have in common? They are Guinness World Records records!

A world record is an amazing achievement that is a fact. It can be a skill someone has, such as being able to blow the largest bubble gum bubble. It can be an interesting fact from nature, such as which bird is the smelliest bird. Guinness World Records has judges who set rules to make sure that all record setters and record breakers follow the same steps. Then, the adjudicators (judges) count, weigh, measure, or compare to make sure that the achievement is the greatest in the world.

So, can you be a Guinness World Records record breaker? If you can run, hop, toss, or even race with an egg on a spoon, you just might see your name on a Guinness World Records Certificate someday. With the help of an adult, visit *www.guinnessworldrecords.com*. There you will find a world of exciting records to explore—and maybe break!

 The Carson-Dellosa Team

Spring-Loaded

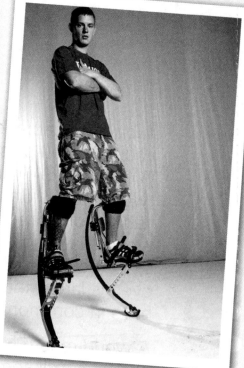

Longest Somersault on Spring-Loaded Stilts
June 18, 2009

Power stilts can really get a person flying through the air! An athlete straps these high-tech wonders to his shoes. The curved shape and springs get the athlete bouncing around in no time. And, this record holder makes it look so easy! John Simkins (UK) wore spring-loaded stilts to help him make the longest somersault. It was 16 feet 6 inches (5.04 m) long! He set the record on the set of a Guinness World Records TV special in Beijing, China. Simkins is no stranger to somersaults on spring-loaded stilts. He has even made leaps over cars with the stilts attached to his feet. The stilts raise Simkins so high off the ground that he is higher than the car before he makes his leap!

● These rabbits were so busy doing somersaults that the numbers they were carrying got mixed up! Unscramble each set of numbers and put them in order to make an addition problem. Be sure to use every number. Sometimes an answer will include one or more two-digit numbers, like 11 + 4 = 15.

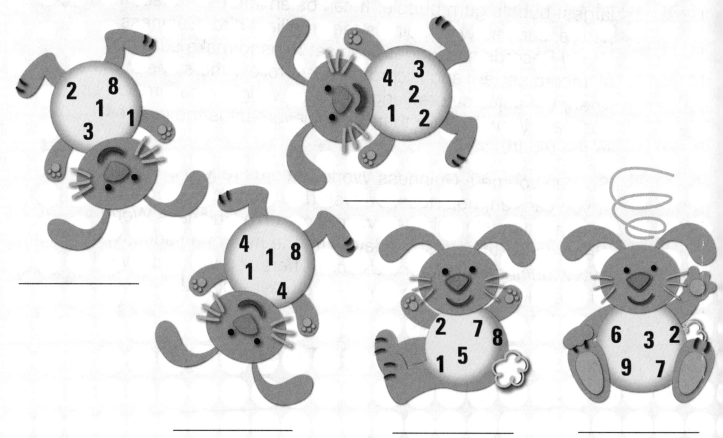

Smart Geese

Largest Game of Duck Duck Goose
September 5, 2005

Have you ever played the game Duck Duck Goose? You may have called it "The Mush Pot," "Peske," or "Antoakyire," depending on where you are from. And, you may think Duck Duck Goose is a game just for kids. But, it's not. In 2005, 1,415 college students and staff at the University of Guelph (Canada) played a record-breaking game of Duck Duck Goose. Record breaking and record setting are nothing new for these students though. At the beginning of every school year, Guelph students try to set and break new world records.

Here are the rules of Duck Duck Goose:

- Everyone sits in a big circle.

- The person who is *It* walks around the outside of the circle.

- *It* taps each person on the head and says, "duck."

- When tapping some person, *It* decides to say, "goose."

- That person is *the Goose*.

- *The Goose* jumps up and chases *It* around the circle.

- The last person back to *the Goose*'s old place in the circle is the new *It*.

- Geese are usually *larger* than ducks. Every item named in the *Smaller* list can be paired with a similar item named in the *Larger* list. But, the item in the *Larger* list must be bigger than the item in the *Smaller* list. The *Larger* words are numbered. Match the words in both lists by writing the correct *Larger* number beside the matching *Smaller* word.

Smaller (such as Duck)		Larger (such as Goose)	
baby	—	1	adult
cat	—	2	bench
chair	—	3	buffalo
cow	—	4	city
hummingbird	—	5	couch
lake	—	6	eagle
mouse	—	7	Earth
North America	—	8	grape
pony	—	9	horse
raisin	—	10	lion
stool	—	11	ocean
stream	—	12	rat
town	—	13	river
worm	—	14	snake

Carry That Weight

Fastest 20 Meters Carrying 300 Kilograms on the Shoulders
April 18, 2009

Agris Kazelniks (Latvia) ran 65.5 feet (20 m) in 11.40 seconds. That's pretty fast, right? Well, he did it while carrying 661 pounds (300 kg) on his shoulders! That would stop most people in their tracks. But, that would not stop Kazelniks. The record holder before this was Kazelniks himself! He beat his own record. After setting the world record in 2005, he continued training so that he could beat his own record in 2009. Kazelniks works hard to compete as a strongman. He trains two hours a day for four days a week. And, he needs a lot of energy to lift that much weight. His normal breakfast is four eggs and three sandwiches! For the rest of the day, he eats meat, potatoes, pasta, and salads. And, he puts every bit of that energy to work!

● Each weight has three numbers on it. Use the numbers on the weights to complete the math problems. Use each number only once for each problem.

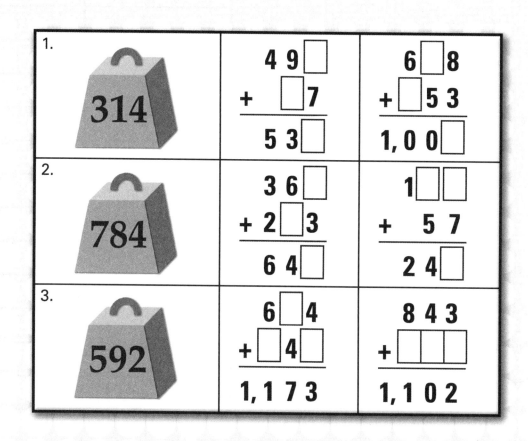

1. 314

```
  4 9 ☐        6 ☐ 8
+   ☐ 7      + ☐ 5 3
―――――――      ―――――――
  5 3 ☐      1,0 0 ☐
```

2. 784

```
  3 6 ☐        1 ☐ ☐
+ 2 ☐ 3      +   5 7
―――――――      ―――――――
  6 4 ☐        2 4 ☐
```

3. 592

```
  6 ☐ 4        8 4 3
+ ☐ 4 ☐      + ☐ ☐ ☐
―――――――      ―――――――
1,1 7 3      1,1 0 2
```

CD-104549

Just Floating Along

Largest Raft Race
July 26, 2009

What would it take to have the world's Largest Raft Race? It would take a lot of rafts and a whole lot of people! You would need 543 rafts and 1,086 people to be exact. Each year, a rubber boat and rafting championship happens in Morioka, Iwate, Japan. In 2009, the championship was better than ever. The part of the championship called the Time Race was used to set the world record. Each raft was timed to see how long it took to finish the course on the Kitakamigawa River. About 50 rafts took off at a time, with each group leaving about five minutes apart. The

race started with 1,452 people in 726 rafts. However, hundreds of rafts were taken out of the race for various reasons. It is important to follow all of the rules when trying to set a world record.

● If each group of 50 rafts took off five minutes apart, about how long did it take for all of the original 726 rafts to take off? Use the raft to show your work.

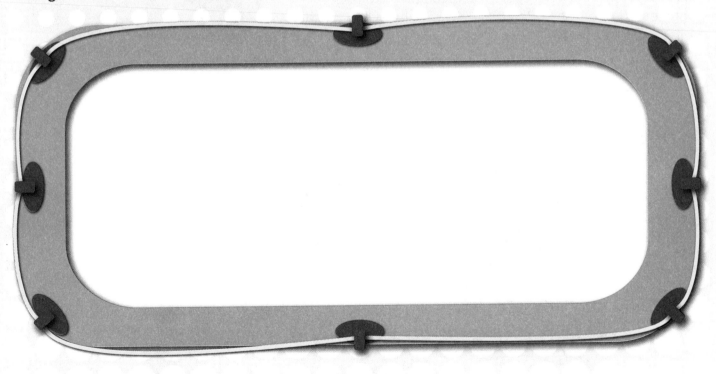

1. What is the answer in hours and minutes? _____

2. What is the answer in only minutes? _____

CD-104549

Earliest Amputee to Win a Summer X Games Gold Medal
July 31, 2009

Chris Ridgway (USA) is a gold medal athlete. "All I ever wanted was to be a pro motocrosser," he says. He began racing bikes at the age of five. By 1992, Ridgway had turned professional. For 10 years, he was living his motocross dream. Then, his legs were so badly broken in a bike crash that he ended up in a wheelchair. Ridgway didn't stop racing though. He found that the pain was less severe while riding his bike than while trying to walk. But, by 2002, the pain grew so fierce that he chose to have his left leg amputated. Even that didn't stop the racer. Ridgway got back on his bike, this time with a prosthetic leg. "This is the hand I was dealt," he says. "I've just got to deal with it." And, deal with it he certainly did! Since then, Ridgway has won four gold medals at the Extremity Games for disabled athletes. In 2009, he took home the gold in the X Games Moto X Super X Adaptive event. Since the amputation, Ridgway has actually taken on another professional sport. He races off-road rock buggies! "I ride," says Ridgway. "Always have and always will."

● Following your dream may take a lot of time and a lot of work. Starting with the phrase *AMPUTEE ATHLETE*, follow the instructions on the next page to discover Ridgway's dream accomplishment.

1. Replace PUT with HOLD. _____

2. Copy the last letter to the beginning of the first word. _____

3. Change all H's to S's. _____

4. Reverse the letters in the last word. _____

5. Exchange the last two vowels. _____

6. Move the last letter of the first word to the fourth position of the first word. _____

7. Move the last letter of the first word to the first position of the last word. _____

8. Replace the third E with M. _____

9. Change OLD to GOLD. _____

10. Move the last letter of the last word to the first position of the first word. _____

11. Change the first T to D. _____

12. Add i after the second L. _____

13. Replace any EE with X   G. _____

14. Split the nine-letter word into two words, starting at the first repeated letter.

_____

Fists That Teach

Fastest Martial Arts Punch
June 14, 2008

The world's fastest fist belongs to John Ozuna (USA). This karate master holds the record for the Fastest Martial Arts Punch. A quick jab with his left hand clocks in at a speed of 43.3 miles (69.6 km) per hour. Ozuna doesn't use his fists to fight. He uses them to teach. Master Ozuna has been teaching martial arts for almost 30 years. His students are as young as 3 and as old as 80. Ozuna's goal is to help these students become the best that they can be. His karate school has a special program that teaches children about safety and self-defense. Ozuna practices a type of karate called *Bok-Fu-Do*, or "The System of the White Tiger." *Bok-Fu-Do* was inspired by many different forms of martial arts from all over the world. This type of karate teaches not only the body but also the mind.

● "Zhi, Yong, Cheng, Ren" is *Bok-Fu-Do*'s motto. Use the clues and the mini-crossword puzzles below to figure out this motto's English translation. Then, write the English words.

___ ___ ___ ___ ___ ___, ___ ___ ___ ___ ___ ___ ___ ___, ___ ___ ___ ___ ___ ___ ___,

___ ___ ___ ___ ___ ___ ___ ___

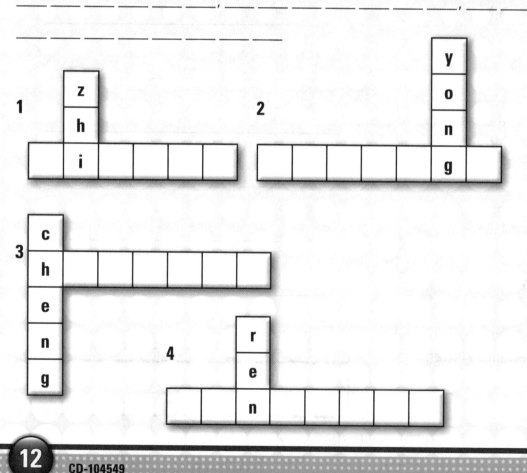

1. If you are wise, you have this (two syllables that rhyme with *his* and *from*).

2. If you are brave, you have this (two syllables that rhyme with *fur* and *edge*).

3. If you are truthful, you have this (three syllables that rhyme with *gone*, *bless*, and *me*).

4. If you are good to others, you have this (two syllables that rhyme with *mind* and *chess*).

CD-104549

Super Arrows

Fastest Time to Shoot 10 Arrows
June 4, 2006

Luis Caídas Martín (Spain) is the fastest shooter in the world—the fastest shooter of arrows, that is. He shot 10 arrows in 1 minute, 7 seconds. That's 6.7 seconds per arrow. Martín shot the arrows on the set of a Guinness World Records show in Madrid, Spain.

The art of archery was first used in hunting, but it is now a sport. A bow and arrow must be used together very precisely to hit a target. The shooter pulls back the bowstring with the arrow in place. When he releases the bowstring, the arrow shoots straight forward. Precision and aim are the name of the game.

● The arrows below form equations in Roman numerals. Look at the key to find what each Roman numeral means. Remove one arrow in each equation to make the equation true. Keep the operation and equal sign the same. Write the new equation in the box.

| = 1 || = 2 ||| = 3 |V = 4   V = 5   V| = 6   V|| = 7   V||| = 8 |X = 9   X = 10

1. V|| + ||| = |X

2. |X − V| = |V

3. V + ||| = V||

CD-104549

Birdie Bath

Longest Marathon Playing Badminton (Singles)
August 23–24, 2009

Can you imagine playing ___adminton for an entire d___y? Not the sor___ of lazy day where you wander over to the badmin___on court and goof around unti___ dinnertim___. But, the 24-hour-straight kin___ of day. F___r 24 hou___s, 5 minutes, 32 s___conds, William ten Zijthoff ___nd Johan Drenthen (both Netherlands) batted a badminton birdie back a___d forth across a net. They di___n't let sleep or blisters ___top them until they ___ad set a new world record. What was the best so___nd they heard during their ordeal? ___hat final whis___le! Ten Zijthoff and Drenthen p___ayed for fun, but they also raised mon___y for the Foundation for Handi___apped Sp___rts. After playing for so long, what did these athletes de___ide to do next? Soa___ their feet in a hot bath!

● Some of the letters in the story above are hidden by badminton birdies. The missing letters spell the name of the child's game that grew to become the badminton game we play today. Fill in the missing letters above. Then, write them in order on the lines below to find the name of the game.

___ ___ ___ ___ ___ ___ ___ ___ ___ ___ ___ ___

___ ___ ___ ___ ___ ___ ___ ___ ___ ___

Play Ball!

Longest Marathon Playing WIFFLE® Ball
August 22–23, 2008

Some ball games go into overtime. But, some *really* go into overtime! The Longest Marathon Playing WIFFLE Ball lasted 24 hours. Ten players total were in the game, with five on each team. The marathon's leader was Benjamin Brozich (USA). The teams played the marathon game at Northwestern High School in Albion, Pennsylvania. The two teams were called the Blues and the Whites. After 149 innings, the final score was Whites 935 and Blues 514. WIFFLE ball rules are similar to those in baseball, but the ball itself is the most important part of the game. A WIFFLE ball has holes in it. This is important because having holes keeps the ball from traveling too far when hit. The air flowing through the ball also creates a lot of curve balls! The sport was developed for use in crowded places, such as cities, and is good for indoor gymnasium play.

● It always helps to practice before playing ball! Carlos, Alvin, Jamie, Jerry, and Kori are on a team together. Make a list to show the possible combinations of one-on-one catch for these team members. The first two combinations have been done for you.

Team Member 1	Team Member 2
Carlos	Alvin
Carlos	Jamie

1. How many different possible ways can the team members play one-on-one catch?

_____

_____

_____

2. How many of the possible combinations include either Alvin or Kori?

_____

_____

_____

CD-104549

Lady Lunger

Fastest Lunge Mile (Female)
November 6, 2005

Dorothea Voegeli (Switzerland) is a long-distance runner. She considers a 26-mile (42-km) marathon to be a short race. Voegeli specializes in the ultramarathon. She runs hundreds of miles. But, in 2005, this champion runner was quite happy to cross the finish line after completing just one mile (1.6 km). Why is that so? She was happy because she wasn't actually running. She was lunging! She put one long step forward, placed a knee to the ground, and switched legs. Then, she repeated this movement at least 1,200 times as quickly and accurately as she could. Voegeli holds the record for the fastest time for a woman to lunge a mile, clocking in at 37 minutes, 58 seconds.

● Runners such as Voegeli compete in many types of races. Below is a list of a few of these events. Some of the letters are missing. Write the missing letters. Then, use them to form three new words so that you can complete Voegeli's inspirational quote.

24-hour ru□

48-h□ur run

1,000-□ile (1,609 km) run

700-m□le (1,127 km) run

10-da□ run

100-kilometer (62-mile) ru□

mar□thon

"____ ____ ____ thing is possible.   ____ ____ thing is ____ ____ possible."

Nasal Ball Spin

Longest Duration Spinning a Basketball on the Nose
February 13, 2010

With training, a seal can balance a ball on his nose. But, can he balance and spin the ball at the same time? That's Shane "Scooter" Christensen's (USA) claim to fame. Christensen is a member of the Harlem Globetrotters. The Globetrotters travel the world entertaining people with their trick-filled basketball games. At the NBA All-Star Jam Session in 2010, Christensen spun a basketball on the tip of his nose for 5.1 seconds. What's the trick? "Find the center [and] spin the ball as straight as you can." He also says he does, of course, do "a lot of practicing, man—hours and hours of practice."

● Here are some things Christensen says about his job as a Harlem Globetrotter. Some of the words have been replaced with other words that rhyme. Read the sentences and write the correct words in the blanks provided.

1. The **tall** ___ ___ ___ ___ is probably in my **sands** ___ ___ ___ ___ ___ 24 hours a
   way ___ ___ ___ .

2. I just **pry** ___ ___ ___ to be creative.

3. You have to **glow** ___ ___ ___ ___ the basics of basketball before trying **sticks**
   ___ ___ ___ ___ ___ .

4. I'm **cart** ___ ___ ___ ___ of the Globetrotters Smile Patrol™—I visit hospitalized children.

5. Visiting children is probably **wetter** ___ ___ ___ ___ ___ ___ than actually **staying**
   ___ ___ ___ ___ ___ ___ the **tame** ___ ___ ___ ___ .

6. We try to **peach** ___ ___ ___ ___ ___ **bids** ___ ___ ___ ___ to be healthy, eat
   healthy.

7. I've traveled all over [the world] and **teen** ___ ___ ___ ___ all
   forts ___ ___ ___ ___ ___ of people.

8. I'm doing something I **glove** ___ ___ ___ ___ to do.

9. I consider the guys on the **beam** ___ ___ ___ ___ to be my
   others ___ ___ ___ ___ ___ ___ ___ .

10. You can **range** ___ ___ ___ ___ ___ ___ a person's life with a
    mile ___ ___ ___ ___ ___ .

CD-104549

Liftoff!

Most Skateboard Nollies in 30 Seconds
August 1, 2009

The Summer X Games is an annual sporting event that focuses on action sports including skateboarding. At the 2009 Los Angeles, California, games, Ivan Sebastian Cordova (USA) proved that he is a skateboarding wonder. In just half a minute, or 30 short seconds, he performed 15 nollies! That's one nollie every two seconds. What is a nollie anyway? It's a skateboarding jump that takes a lot of skill to perform. Ivan uses his front foot to pop the skateboard nose down to the ground. At the same time, he uses his back foot to scrape the skateboard backward. When these two moves are combined, the skateboard achieves major liftoff!

● Cordova's world record can follow a pattern of 2 nollies in 4 seconds. The *input* row is the number of nollies. The *output* row is the number of seconds it takes to do that many nollies. Fill in the chart to complete the pattern.

Number of nollies	2	4		8		12	14		18
Seconds			12		20			32	

Now, complete this input chart and figure out the rule.

Number of nollies	3	4		6	7
Seconds	9		15		

Rule: _____

CD-104549

Soft Snowball or Snow Softball?

Largest Snow Softball Tournament
March 6–8, 2009

Softball is a warm-weather sport, right? Maybe it's not! What if you pitch snowballs instead of softballs? Then, you can play all winter long! And, no better reason exists to throw snowballs than to help needy families. In 1999, friends in Barre, Vermont (USA), organized a snow softball tournament. They called it Freezing Fun for Families. This event raised money for a local family with a child who was battling cancer. Eight teams participated. By 2009, the fund-raiser had grown to 61 teams and 795 players. The tournament set a Guinness World Records record for the Largest Snow Softball Tournament ever. Today, Freezing Fun for Families continues to grow. It has raised thousands of dollars to help children and their families. What a wonderful snowball effect!

● Two scrambled Freezing Fun for Families words are at each base in the softball diamond. Every word is missing one letter. The snowballs inside the diamond contain the missing letters. Match the snowballs with the correct words and write the unscrambled words in the spaces provided.

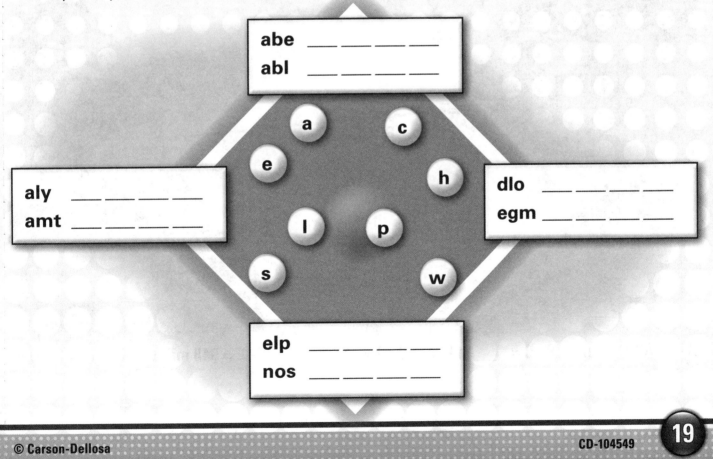

abe ___ ___ ___ ___

abl ___ ___ ___ ___

a   c

e   h

l   p

aly ___ ___ ___ ___

amt ___ ___ ___ ___

dlo ___ ___ ___ ___

egm ___ ___ ___ ___

s   w

elp ___ ___ ___ ___

nos ___ ___ ___ ___

Keep On Paddling!

Longest Paddleboard Journey by a Team
August 28, 2009

Three women earned the record for the Longest Paddleboard Journey by a Team. Stephanie Geyer-Barneix, Alexandra Lux, and Flora Manciet (all France) worked together to cross the Atlantic Ocean. They set out to travel a total of 3,201 miles (5,151 km) from Breton, Canada, to Capbreton, France. Their journey took them 54 days to complete. Many types of paddleboards are meant for someone to stand on. The paddler usually moves the board with a paddle. The women who set this record used paddleboards that allowed them to sit or kneel on the boards. They paddled with their hands. The women took turns paddling in a nonstop relay-race-style trek across the ocean. Crews were with them to let the women get on and off of the paddleboards.

● A group of paddleboarders divided their journey into 5 parts. But, the total distance for one of the legs of the journey is missing. Look at the map to see the distance of each part of the journey. Then, find the distance of the missing part if the whole journey were a 3,201-mile trip.

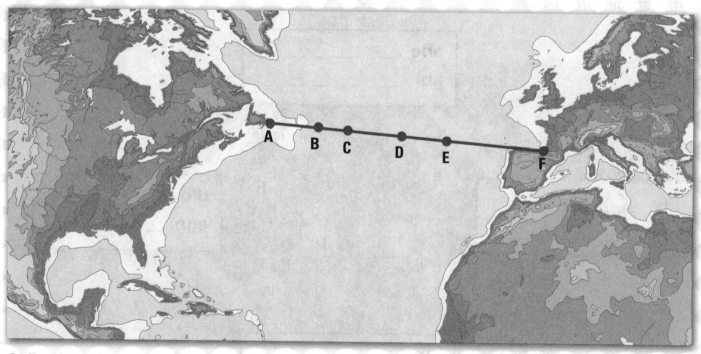

A–B = 684 miles   **B–C = _____ miles**   **C–D = 717 miles**   **D–E = 548 miles**   **E–F = 761 miles**

Hockey Hero

Oldest Hockey Player (Female)
March 7, 2009

At the age of 74, Anne Graves (UK) earned the record for being the Oldest Hockey Player (Female) ever. Although many of her teammates are decades younger, Graves's age is nothing compared to the age of the sport. Field hockey is one of the oldest competitive games in the world. No one really knows where it started. Ancient drawings date it back thousands of years. Today, it is a sport played around the world.

You have to have skill, speed, and endurance to play field hockey. Graves joined her local hockey club when she was 18. She has been playing ever since. "I used to be a decent player," she says, "but I wish I had a faster pair of legs now!" Graves's hockey legs must still be pretty strong. In her 2008–2009 season, she played 14 games in her usual role—team captain.

● Field hockey is probably one of the first stick-and-ball games. The stick is hooked, and the ball is round. The first modern field hockey team was formed in mid-nineteenth-century England. The game had few rules, and the ball was a strange shape that is not what you see today. Answer the following clues. Your answers, from top to bottom, will spell the shape of this first field hockey ball.

___ ___ ___ ___

The third letter of the second word in this sport's name

The letter representing "United" in the abbreviation for "United Kingdom"

The first letter of the most important piece of equipment that goes with "stick"

The vowel that appears the most times in Graves's record title

A Hop, a Skip, and a Jump

Most Skips Double Dutch Style in One Minute
May 3, 2009

People all over the world jump rope. Some do it for exercise. Some do it for fun. And, some do it to become famous. In 2009, Nobuyoshi Ando (Japan) set a world record in speed skipping. He double Dutch skip-jumped 202 times in one minute. Double Dutch is a jump rope game where two ropes are turned together like eggbeaters. The jumper has to hop over the ropes without becoming tangled. The ropes make a slapping sound as they hit the ground. To help the jumper keep this rhythm, skipping games include chants. Children everywhere have created their own chants in their own languages.

"Salt and Vinegar, Mustard, Pepper" is a traditional British skipping chant. If you speak these words in a certain way, they create a distinctive rhythm. The uppercase syllables are accented; the lowercase syllables are not.

SALT *and*
VIN*egar*
MUS*tard*
PEP*per*

● The words in this chant are names of things you might add to food. Below are eight titled boxes. For each box, choose four words that have something to do with the title. Think of your rhythm. Write those words in the boxes. The boxed title letters, in order, will spell the Japanese word for rope jumping.

___ ___ ___ ___ ___ ___ ___

FRIE**N**DS	PL**A**CES	**W**EATHER	VAC**A**TION
_____	_____	_____	_____
_____	_____	_____	_____
_____	_____	_____	_____
_____	_____	_____	_____

SPOR**T**S	FO**O**D	**B**IRDS	FAM**I**LY
_____	_____	_____	_____
_____	_____	_____	_____
_____	_____	_____	_____
_____	_____	_____	_____

CD-104549

Race to the Top

Oldest Person to Climb Mount Everest (Male)
May 25, 2008

What is it like to be the oldest person to reach the highest point on Earth? Ask Min Bahadur Sherchan (Nepal). He reached the summit of Mount Everest at age 76 years, 340 days. That's less than a month short of his 77th birthday. But, it was a race to the top! The very next day, Yuichiro Miura from Japan reached the top of Mount Everest at age 75 years, 227 days. He was the second-oldest person to climb the world's highest mountain. Dangerous climbs and freezing conditions make the trip very difficult. Climbers suffer sickness from being at such high altitudes. Climbing Mount Everest is a challenge at any age!

● Five children all finished a hike one at a time. Use the clues to list the children in the order that they finished.

| Jan | Olivia | Leo | Maggie | Mario |

Jan finished before Leo but after Maggie.

Olivia finished after Mario.

Leo finished before Mario but after Jan.

| _____ | _____ | _____ | _____ | _____ |
| first | second | third | fourth | fifth |

CD-104549

Keep on Leaping!

Most Vaults in One Hour
May 9, 2009

For some people, just one flight over a vault can be a challenge. But, it is not a challenge for the Blue Falcons Gymnastic Display Team (UK). The team vaulted 6,250 times in just one hour! The 10-member team was from Chelmer Valley High School. The boys set their record at the Meadows Shopping Center in Chelmsford, Essex. To make the vaults, the teens ran one at a time toward a device called a "table," or a "vault." A leap onto a springboard got them flying into the air toward the table. They reached for and touched the table. Then, they pushed themselves over the table to land on the other side. The team kept a constant run of jumps and leaps for 60 minutes.

● Four children started a vaulting team. Each child did 15, 26, 35, or 39 vaults in one hour. Use the clues and the table to find the number of vaults each child did. Write the answers in the chart.

1. Sean did more than twice the number of vaults as another vaulter with the same number of letters in his name.

2. Gavin did fewer vaults than Sean.

3. The vaulter with the longest name won a trophy.

	15	26	35	39
Rachel				
Sean				
Gavin				
Owen				

Lumber-Jackie?

Most Women's Logrolling World Championships 2003

Tina Bosworth (USA) is the most famous female logroller in the world. By 2003, she had won the World Lumberjack Championship an amazing 10 times! Logrolling is not an easy sport. You must be quick on your feet. You must have good balance. And, you should be able to swim! That's because logrolling takes place in deep water.

Bosworth wears spiked shoes to help grip the log. Once she and her competitor are standing and balanced at opposite ends of the log, they try to knock each other off into the water. They do this by moving their feet to make the log spin. Running forward is called a "front step." Running backward is called a "back step" and is more difficult. A bucking match is when the two competitors fight for the logrolling direction. One runs forward while the other runs backward. This often results in a fall by one or both of the logrollers. The key to being a champion logroller is to never take your eyes off your competitor's feet!

● A logroller such as Bosworth is called a "birler." A male birler is a type of lumberjack. Below is a log covered in letters. Knock off any letters that are *not* found in the words BIRLER and LUMBERJACK. The letters remaining on the log will spell, in order, the proper name for a female lumberjack.

__ __ __ __ __ __ __ __ __

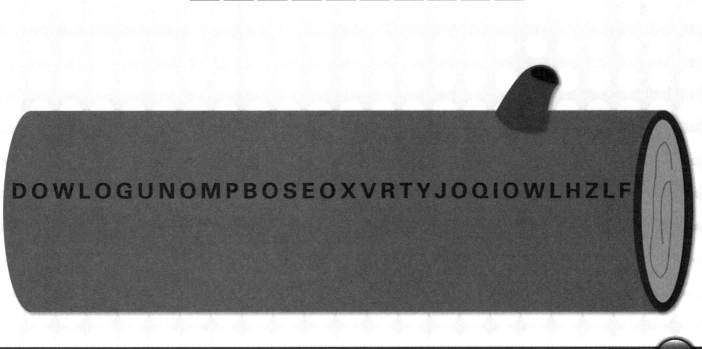

DOWLOGUNOMPBOSEOXVRTYJOQIOWLHZLF

Up, Up, and Away on One Wheel

Longest Jump on a Unicycle
September 16, 2006

Who can jump a distance of almost 10 feet (3 m) in one bound? David Weichenberger (Austria) can—on his unicycle! Weichenberger is a world champion unicyclist. He competes in freestyle, trials, and "muni," which is short for "mountain unicycling." He is one of the fastest unicyclists in the world. In 2006, a teenage Weichenberger jumped a record-breaking distance of 9 feet 8 inches (2.95 m) on his unicycle. Weichenberger has been a unicycle rider since he was 11 years old. He first started unicycling while juggling. Both require athleticism and artistry. Weichenberger loves to perform. He also loves to challenge himself.

___ ___ □ ___ ___ ___

8 feet (2.4 m)
"I am a type of mammal that has long ears."

___ ___ □ ___ ___ ___ ___ ___ ___ ___

3 feet (0.9 m)
"I am a type of insect that is large and green."

___ □ ___ ___ ___

___ ___ ___ ___ ___ ___ ___ ___ ___ ___ ___

9 feet 8 inches (2.95 m)
"I am the world record holder of the Longest Jump on a Unicycle."

___ ___ ___ ___

15 feet (4.6 m)
"I am a type of amphibian."

___ ___ □ ___ ___ ___ ___ ___

35 feet (10.7 m)
"I am a type of mammal that has a pocket."

● The blank lines hold the names of some animals that jump. Some can jump a distance that is less than Weichenberger's record leap. Others can jump farther. Using the clues and the spaces provided, write the names of the missing animals. The boxed letters, in order, will spell the most important key to unicycling.

___ ___ L ___ ___ CE

CD-104549

Great Shot!

Longest Golf Shot While Seated
November 27, 2009

Dale Sheppard (Australia) took one long swing at a golf ball on the 11th hole in Mornington Peninsula in Victoria, Australia. And, what's amazing is that he did it while sitting in a wheelchair. He hit the shot during a charity golf day. The event raised money for people with disabilities. The distance was measured from the place Sheppard hit the ball to the place the ball first landed. That distance was 372 feet 6 inches (113.55 m). Even after the record was set, the ball continued to bounce and roll. It traveled another 99 feet 5 inches (30.3 m). What a shot!

● Three golfers hit a golf ball a long distance. Add the amounts the balls flew through the air plus the amount they bounced and rolled on the ground. Which golfer hit the ball that traveled the longest total distance?

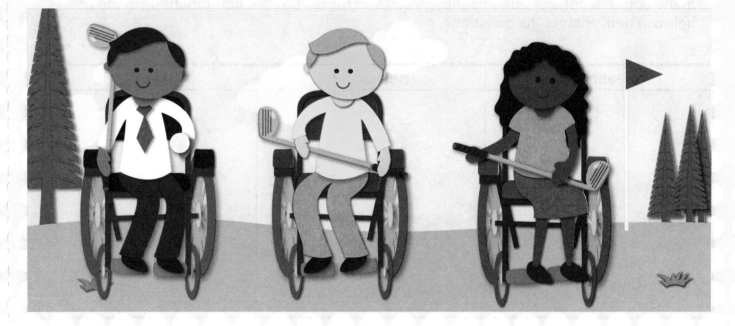

Hugo

311 feet 11 inches
77 feet 8 inches
total _____

Graham

289 feet 8 inches
99 feet 10 inches
total _____

Alexis

367 feet 3 inches
101 feet 6 inches
total _____

The Art of Joggling

Fastest 10K Joggling with Three Objects (Male)
September 10, 2006

When was the last time you saw a joggling competition? Even more important, what is joggling? It is the fine art of jogging while juggling! Michal Kapral (Canada) jogged a distance of 6.2 miles (10 km) in 36 minutes, 27 seconds. The amazing part is that he was juggling three beanbags the whole time without dropping them! Kapral is one of the world's most talented jogglers. He even holds a world record for running the fastest joggling marathon. And, he set that record while chewing gum! In the past, Kapral also held another joggling world record. It was for the fastest joggling marathon while pushing a baby stroller. Kapral seems to have no trouble getting a lot of things done at once!

● A joggler has a red, a green, a blue, and a yellow beanbag. She can only use three of the beanbags during a race. How many combinations of three beanbags can she make? List the combinations in the chart below. Then, answer the questions.

Beanbag 1	Beanbag 2	Beanbag 3

1. How many combinations include a yellow beanbag? _____

2. If the joggler must always start by throwing a yellow beanbag in the air, how many possible combinations are there? _____

Here Comes the Iron Man!

Arm Curls, Most Weight in One Hour
October 5, 2007

Eamonn Keane (Ireland) sure likes lifting weights! Holding a 48.5-pound (22-kg) weight in one hand, he did 1,058 arm curls in just one hour. If you add the weight of all of those arm curls, the amount of weight he lifted during that hour was a whopping 51,314.8 pounds (23,276 kg)! Keane holds a total of seven Guinness World Records records in the strength category. His other records include Most Weight Bench-Pressed in One Hour. Keane also lifted the Most Weight by Dumbbell Rows in One Hour. With seven titles, it is no wonder Keane has earned the nickname "the Iron Man."

● The turtle below does arm curls very slowly. He can do only 3 arm curls every minute. But, the turtle never slows down, and he never needs a break. Complete the chart to show how many arm curls the turtle can do over time. Practice your math stamina!

Minutes	1	5	10	20	40	80	160	320	640	1,280
Curls	3									

"Travel" Soccer Tricks

Most Around the World Ball Control Tricks in One Minute (Male)
October 3, 2008

John Farnworth (UK) "traveled" around the world an unbelievable 85 times in a single minute. Of course, he didn't really travel anywhere. But, his foot did! Around the World is a difficult ball trick. While keeping the soccer ball in the air, Farnworth spins his kicking foot around the bouncing ball without letting the ball touch the ground. Doing one successful Around the World is difficult. Doing 85 is phenomenal! Farnworth is a world champion soccer freestyler. He performs tricks with a ball while keeping it constantly in the air. He uses different parts of his body, except his hands. Using the hands is against soccer rules. Farnworth flips and twists and never lets the ball drop to the ground.

Farnworth grew up with a ball practically glued to his feet. He developed great fancy foot skills. He became interested in soccer freestyle as a teenager. Now a young man, Farnworth really does travel around the world, promoting and teaching freestyle. Soccer freestyle is an art form. Both athletes and artists need to work hard to stay at the top of their games. Farnworth trains at least 40 hours per week to perfect and improve his freestyle skills.

● The soccer balls on the next page contain words related to soccer freestyle. The words are disguised in a code. The numbers 1 to 26 each represent one letter of the alphabet. Decode the words and write them on the lines. The boxed letters, in order, will spell the name of another common freestyle game.

___ ___ ___ ___ ___   ___ ___ ___ ___

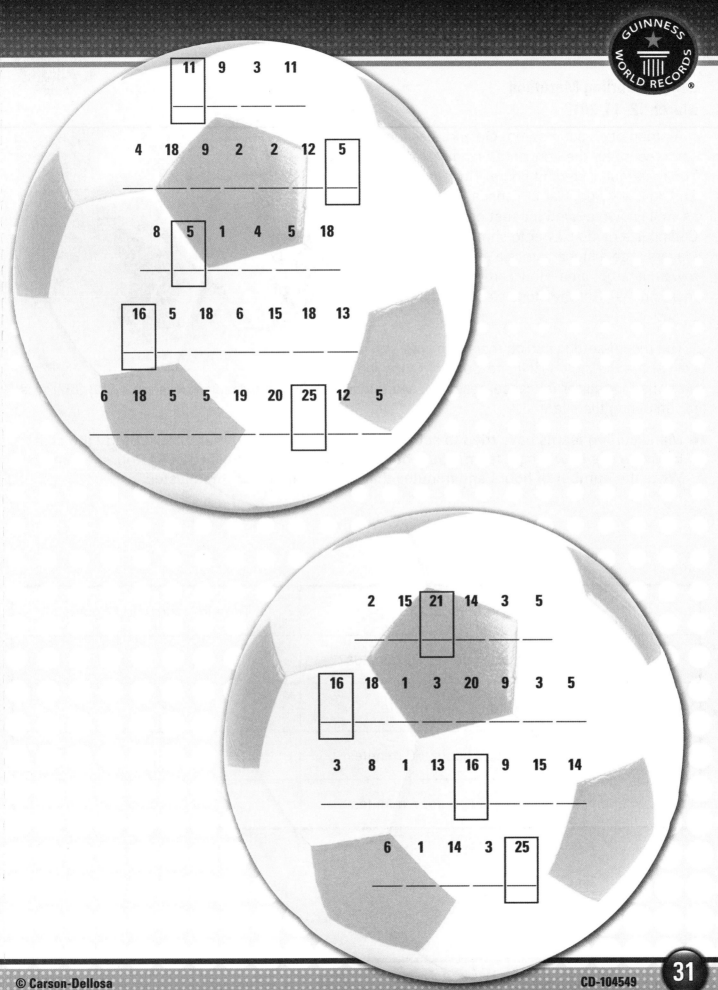

11 9 3 11
___ ___ ___ ___

4 18 9 2 2 12 5
___ ___ ___ ___ ___ ___ ___

8 5 1 4 5 18
___ ___ ___ ___ ___ ___

16 5 18 6 15 18 13
___ ___ ___ ___ ___ ___ ___

6 18 5 5 19 20 25 12 5
___ ___ ___ ___ ___ ___ ___ ___ ___

2 15 21 14 3 5
___ ___ ___ ___ ___ ___

16 18 1 3 20 9 3 5
___ ___ ___ ___ ___ ___ ___ ___

3 8 1 13 16 9 15 14
___ ___ ___ ___ ___ ___ ___ ___

6 1 14 3 25
___ ___ ___ ___ ___

Longest Curling Marathon
March 12–14, 2010

A group of 10 curlers from Ontario, Canada, set a record for the Longest Curling Marathon. The marathon lasted 54 hours, 1 minute! Curling is very popular in Canada, but it is not as well known around the rest of the world. Curling is a game similar to shuffleboard. Players slide a stone across a sheet of ice toward a target area. How can you earn more points? Get the stone closer to the target!

The record-setting curling marathon was held at the Burlington Golf and Country Club. The event was part of a fund-raiser for cancer research. More than $28,000 in Canadian dollars (US$28,397) was raised during the event.

● Many curling teams have tried to set world records for curling marathons. Study the chart below to see how long a team would have to curl to beat the record of 54 hours, 1 minute. Write the number of hours and minutes that each curling marathon lasted.

	Time Spent Curling	Time in Hours and Minutes
Team A	2 days, 3 hours, 70 minutes	
Team B	2 days, 142 minutes	
Team C	2 days, 8 hours, 50 minutes	
Team D	1 day, 29 hours, 7 minutes	

Four-Cross Champ

Most Wins of the Mountain Bike World Championships in Four-Cross (Male) 2007

You are waiting—helmet on—for the signal to start. The tires on your mountain bike are firm and strong. The racetrack is downhill. It is filled with steep jumps and hairpin turns. You are determined to finish the course in record time. The three competitors beside you are as well. Four-cross is a mountain bike speed race between four people. It is you against them. And, by the time you all reach the end of the grueling course, only one person will be the winner!

Brian Lopes (USA) holds the record for the Most Wins of the Mountain Bike World Championships in Four-Cross by a man. He learned to ride a bike at age four and turned professional at age 17. Although he started out as a BMX rider, Lopes took home the top four-cross prize in 2002, 2005, and 2007. Four-cross is a relatively new sport. It is tough, fast, and unpredictable. Because a four-cross course is both downhill and winding, the race is always exciting.

● How much do you know about four-cross? Decide if each statement below is true or false. Then, circle the corresponding answer letter in the table. If you guess correctly, the circled letters, from top to bottom, will spell the nickname of this four-cross champion.

___ ___ ___ ___ ___ 'Brian

True or False?

1. Four-cross is a cycling sport.

2. In four-cross, a racer competes with two other racers.

3. Mountain bikes have heavier tires than racing bikes.

4. A four-cross trail is straight.

5. Four-cross competitors wear helmets.

Four-Cross True or False		
Question	TRUE	FALSE
1	F	T
2	A	L
3	Y	E
4	H	I
5	N	O

Teamwork

Greatest Karting Distance Traveled in 24 Hours
September 21, 2007

Keep on rolling! How can a kart keep moving for 24 hours? It takes teamwork! A motorsport team called Equipe Vitesse set the record for the Greatest Karting Distance Traveled in 24 hours. The team traveled 1,277.97 miles (2,056.7 km)! They set the record on a track in Middlesbrough, United Kingdom. The kart was a Tony Kart Racer EVS fitted with a small car engine. Team members took turns jumping behind the wheel and then speeding off again. The team has worked together for many years and has won many racing events together.

● The path below shows the number of miles the team traveled. However, one leg of the race is missing. Add the sections of the race to figure out which amount is missing. Write your answer on the line.

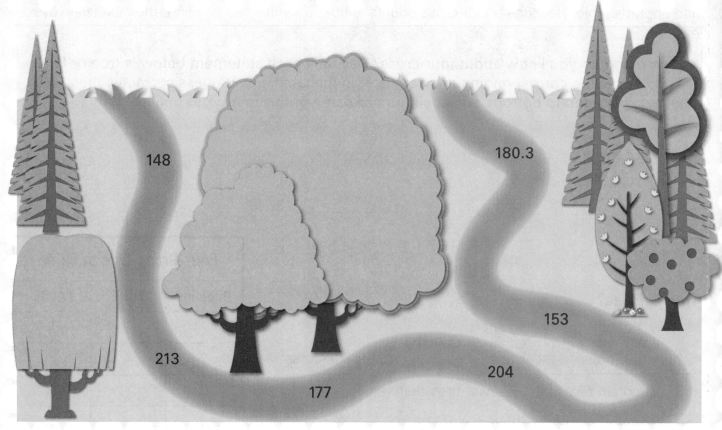

148

180.3

213

177

204

153

_____

Handles and Wheels

Fastest 40 Meters by a Human Wheelbarrow
November 12, 2009

Guinness World Records Day is an annual event when people around the world attempt to set or break world records. Adrian Rodriguez is from Mexico. Sergiy Vetrogonov is from the Ukraine. On Guinness World Records Day in Finland, they set the record for the Fastest 40 Meters (131 feet) by a Human Wheelbarrow. The two men crossed an area almost the width of a football field in just 17 seconds!

It takes two people to make a human wheelbarrow. For this record event, Vetrogonov was the "wheel." He lay on the ground supported only by his hands. Rodriguez held the "handles." He held Vetrogonov's legs up by the ankles. The trick to the human wheelbarrow is for both people to "run" at the same pace. Because one person is running using only his hands, this can be difficult. Often, the "wheel" gets completely run over by the person holding the "handles." But, Vetrogonov and Rodriguez's coordination was perfect. They were another Guinness World Records Day success!

● The words in the word bank are organized alphabetically. They could also be organized into groups of three related words such as *Finland*, *Mexico*, and *Ukraine*. In the spaces provided, rewrite the words in five logical groups of three.

Word Bank

buffalo	human	soccer
day	month	tennis
Earth	planet	wheelbarrow
football	rake	world
fox	shovel	year

_____   _____

_____   _____

_____   _____

_____   _____   _____

_____   _____   _____

_____   _____   _____

Now That's Big!

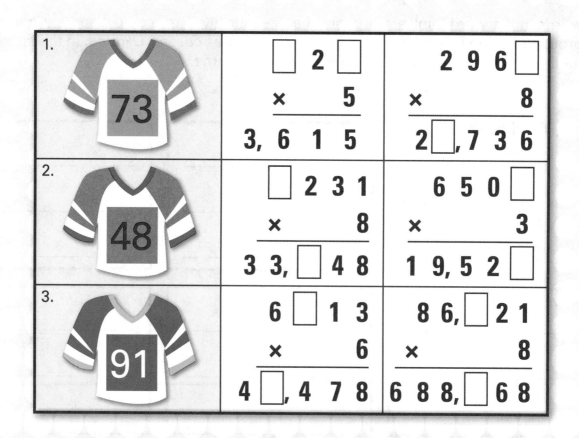

Largest Soccer Shirt
April 5, 2009

Most shirts come in sizes small, medium, large, and extra large. But, what size is a shirt that measures 234 feet 1 inch wide by 259 feet 8 inches (71.35 m x 79.15 m) long? That's beyond extra large. That's huge! A company called AVEA created the shirt for an event in Istanbul, Turkey. To make the shirt, miles of fabric and thread were needed.

So, where can a shirt like this be displayed? It was unveiled at a sports stadium and was spread across the soccer field. Not many other places are big enough to display such a huge shirt that weighs more than 1,000 pounds (453.6 kg)!

● Most soccer shirts have numbers to identify them. Look at the numbers on the shirts below. Use the two numbers on each shirt to complete the pairs of math problems. Use each number only once in each problem.

1. (73)

☐ 2 ☐ × 5 = 3,615	2 9 6 ☐ × 8 = 2☐,736

2. (48)

☐ 2 3 1 × 8 = 33,☐48	6 5 0 ☐ × 3 = 19,52☐

3. (91)

6 ☐ 1 3 × 6 = 4☐,478	8 6,☐ 2 1 × 8 = 688,☐68

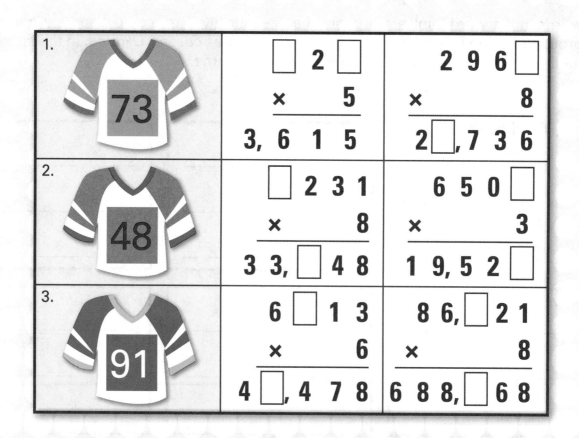

CD-104549

Youngest Rugby Union Referee
November 30, 2008

What was a boy doing on the field during an official girls' rugby match? He was blowing the whistle! In 2008, Harry Goodhew (UK) became the Youngest Rugby Union Referee. How old was he? He was 11 years, 234 days old, which was about the same age as the girls he was refereeing. Harry officiated two games that day. "It went quite smoothly," he said. But, he added, "One coach kept telling me that his girls were being fouled, [so] I had to put him in his place." Harry had just earned his refereeing license that autumn, but he had been playing rugby since he was six. Refereeing was an eye-opener for Harry. "It made me see how difficult it really is for referees at any level to keep law and order."

● Rugby was played in Britain long before it came to America. In rugby, players kick and dribble the ball like in soccer. They also throw and catch the ball like in American football. The puzzle below contains some rugby-related words. Using the word bank, cross out the rugby words as you find them. The unused letters, in order from top to bottom and left to right, will spell the original British word that describes how rugby play restarts after a penalty. The first five letters in this word will also spell a common American rugby term.

___ ___ ___ ___ ___ ___ ___ ___ ___ ___

c	b	l	f	r	u	c	k	f	l	a	t
r	a	c	o	n	v	e	r	s	i	o	n
a	c	s	r	o	e	c	r	e	n	l	u
b	k	r	w	s	p	p	e	v	e	m	g
b	s	m	a	u	l	r	u	e	o	a	o
i	m	h	r	s	o	m	h	n	u	r	a
n	p	a	d	c	h	g	e	s	t	k	l
g	o	b	s	t	r	u	c	t	i	o	n

Word Bank

backs	loop
conversion	mark
crabbing	maul
crash	obstruction
flat	phase
forwards	punt
goal	ruck
heel	sevens
lineout	score

CD-104549

Look, Mom, No Hands!

Longest Distance Cycling with No Hands for One Hour
June 23, 2009

It's difficult for anyone to cycle more than 23 miles (37 km) in one hour. But, Erik Skramstad (USA) did just that! What's even more impressive is that he did it with no hands. He traveled 23.25 miles (37.4 km) at the Las Vegas Motor Speedway in Las Vegas, Nevada. The middle school science teacher rode 62 laps on an oval track that was three-eighths of a mile (0.60 km) long. He made more than 200 left turns on the track with no hands by gently shifting his weight on the bike. Skramstad beat the previous record holder's record by nearly 7 miles (11.3 km). That's some speed and balance all at once!

● Find the bicycle path that is the longest. Start at the center and go along the lines touching five numbers as you go. The line from the fifth number must lead back to where you started in the middle. You may only touch each part of the path once. Draw a line on the path that shows the longest distance in miles.

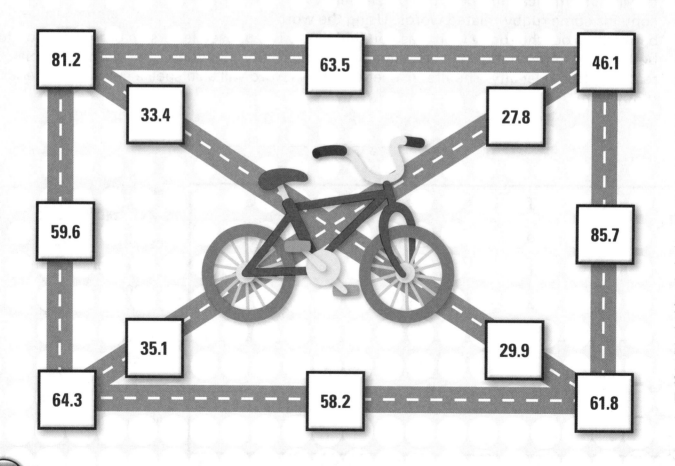

© Carson-Dellosa

Scrambled Eggs

Largest Egg-and-Spoon Race
July 27, 2008

If your school has ever held a field day, you probably know all about egg-and-spoon races. All you need is an ordinary teaspoon and an egg—or maybe two eggs. Maybe you even need a whole carton of eggs! Using the spoon, players continually pass an egg to the next person on the team. If someone drops the egg, the whole team has to start again. The first group to finish is the winner.

In 2008, the Singapore TV show *Record Breakers* held a competition. Schools from around the country competed in record-breaking events. The grand finale was the egg-and-spoon race. More than 1,000 students participated in this event. Nobody counted the number of eggs broken that day, but they did count the number of kids—1,308!

● Below are the names of some other typical field day events. Some of the words are scrambled. Unscramble the words and write them on the lines.

1. a c k s ___ ___ ___ ___   race

2. e h o s ___ ___ ___ ___   scramble

3. e e h r t - d e e g g l _____ - _____   race

4. a b c e l o s t _____   course

5. e e h l w a b o r r w _____   relay

6. a c e e g n r s v _____   hunt

7. a b e n a b g _____   toss

8. a e r t w a b l l n o o _____ _____   toss

9. g u t a r w ___ ___ ___ -of- ___ ___ ___

CD-104549

Prince of the Pins

Most Wins of the Bowling World Cup
1996

Rafael "Paeng" Nepomuceno (Philippines) is the champion of Tenpin bowling. He is so famous in the bowling world that he only goes by one name—Paeng. In 1976, Paeng won his first Bowling World Cup. He was only 19, making him the youngest winner ever. Since then, he has won a total of four World Cup titles and more than 100 international competitions. He continues to be heavily involved in the sport even though many players are half his age. During his long career, five Philippine presidents have honored Paeng. He is practically royalty!

Wooden bowling pins look like old-fashioned milk bottles. Ten of these pins are arranged in a triangle at the end of a long, smooth bowling lane. Paeng throws a heavy bowling ball down the lane toward the pins. The more pins he knocks down and the fewer tries he needs to take to knock them all down, the more points he scores. He is a master at throwing the perfect shot when the pins that are left after his first throw are not close together.

● Bowlers have names for everything. *Barmaid* and *Baby Split* are types of shots. *Cheesecakes* are bowling lanes where bowlers are able to score high points. *Chicken Wing* and *Cranker* are throwing styles. On the next page are six sets of bowling pins. In the sets, some pins have already been knocked down by different types of shots. Bowlers know each of these shots by a special name. Beside each set of pins is a clue to the name. Using the clues and the spaces provided, name all of these shots. The boxed letters from your riddle answers, in order, will spell the name of the shot that every bowler wants to throw.

—— —— —— —— —— ——

CD-104549

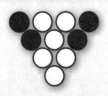
Another word for *large* + What helped Dumbo the elephant fly

___ ___ ___ ___ ___ ___ ___ [ ]

What you have to get to score a point in hockey or soccer + Tall sticks used to mark boundaries

___ ___ ___ ___ ___ ___ [ ] ___ ___

Having a taste like a lemon (not sweet) + A Granny Smith or a golden delicious

___ ___ ___ [ ] ___ ___ ___ ___ ___ ___

Something like a tricycle but with only two wheels

___ [ ] ___ ___ ___ ___ ___ ___

Something your pants may have more than one of

___ ___ ___ [ ] ___ ___ ___

A long, skinny reptile with no legs + The body parts we use to see

___ ___ ___ ___ ___ [ ] ___ ___ ___

CD-104549

Long, Longer, Longest!

Longest Rideable Surfboard
June 12, 2009

It's one thing to have the world's longest surfboard. It's another thing to be able to ride it! In 2009, Rico De Souza (Brazil) hit the waves at Solemar Beach in Espírito Santo, Brazil, to test out his latest surfboard. This one was 30 feet 10 inches long (9.42 m). De Souza holds the previous records for this category. He set those records in 2006 and 2008. De Souza's surfboards are so big that it takes at least five people to carry them onto the beach. His 2009 board was 10 inches (25 cm) longer than his 2008 board. Will he do it again? Time will tell. Surf's up!

● These children made their own surfboards too. But, whose is the longest? Use the clues to find the length of each board. Circle the name of the child with the longest board.

1. Lamar's board is 6 feet 2 inches longer than Rico De Souza's.

2. Charlotte's board is half the length of Lamar's, plus 17 inches.

3. Alfonso's board is 11 feet 5 inches longer than Charlotte's.

4. Terrance's board is 50 percent longer than Lamar's.

Alfonso	Charlotte	Lamar	Terrance

Marathon Mom

Fastest Half Marathon While Pushing a Stroller (Female)
September 15, 2001

Lots of moms run races, including Nancy Schubring (USA). Their families, including their children, usually cheer from the sidelines. In 2001, Schubring ran a half marathon with her toddler tucked in a stroller riding right in front of her! Schubring set a record that day for the Fastest Half Marathon While Pushing a Stroller (Female). They—mom and child—ran the race in 1 hour, 30 minutes, 51 seconds. That's only 25 minutes slower than the time for the fastest half marathon by a woman running all by herself. A race this length is a little more than 13 miles (21 km). That means Schubring's toddler was zipping along with her mother at a speed of about 6.5 miles (10.5 km) per hour.

- The word *marathon* comes from ancient Greece. A messenger ran 26 miles (42 km) between Marathon and a second Greek city to bring news of a victory. Speed was important. Below is a list of animals and their top speeds. Using the word bank and clues, write the missing animal names. The boxed letters, in order, will spell the name of this second Greek city.

__ __ __ __ __ __

	Word Bank	
angelfish giraffe beetle greyhound cheetah ostrich		

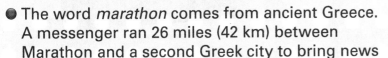

mph	km/h	Animal Names	Clues
3	5	□__ __ __ __ __ __ __	I live in water.
6	9	__ __ __ □ __ __	I have a shell.
33	53	__ __ __ __ __ __ □	I eat meat.
35	56	__ __ __ __ __ __ □	I am very tall.
39	63	__ __ __ __ __ __ □ __ __	I am a good pet.
43	69	__ □ __ __ __ __ __	I cannot fly.

Highest Wall Climb on Darts
November 11, 2009

When you say someone is driving you up a wall, do you really mean it like Maiko Kiesewetter (Germany) means it? He literally climbs the walls! In 2009, he completed the Highest Wall Climb on Darts as a celebration of Guinness World Records Day in Hamburg, Germany. He climbed 16.5 feet (5 m)! It may sound difficult to climb a wall while being held up just by darts. But, Maiko was pretty lightweight. In fact, when he set the record, he was only 13 years old! So, what does Maiko want to be when he grows up? He wants to be a stuntman, of course!

● The three climbing walls below are different shapes. Count the blocks to find the wall that has the most blocks.

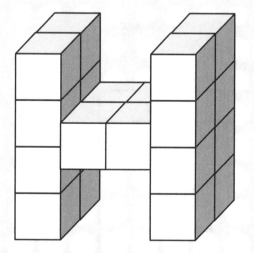

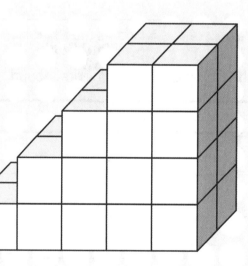

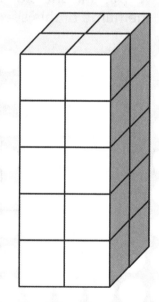

_____ blocks   _____ blocks   _____ blocks

CD-104549

Seated Flips

First Landed Wheelchair Backflip
October 25, 2008

When Aaron Fotheringham (USA) landed a wheelchair backflip in 2008, he set a new Guinness World Records record. According to Guinness World Records, 16-year-old Aaron's flip was the First Landed Wheelchair Backflip ever. That's the official record. But, Aaron had actually been doing wheelchair backflips since he was 14. Aaron uses a wheelchair because his legs don't work. He was born with spina bifida. Having this disease doesn't slow him down. Aaron is an extreme wheelchair athlete. Unofficially, he has completed not just one, but six consecutive wheelchair backflips! Aaron loves to show younger kids how much fun their wheelchairs can be. By performing stunts all over the world, Aaron hopes to help others see their own disabilities in new ways. His goal is to design "the most wicked" wheelchair in the world. What does Aaron call his sport? He calls it "hard-core sitting"!

● Below is a wheel of letters. Cross out any letters that are in the phrase *spina bifida*. Rearrange the remaining letters in the outer wheel to spell Aaron's nickname.

—— —— —— —— —— —— ——

● Rearrange the remaining letters in the inner wheel to spell the name of a piece of equipment Aaron always wears.

—— —— —— —— ——

CD-104549

Keep on Kicking!

Longest Marathon Playing Kickball
April 9–11, 2010

Some people just never get tired of playing kickball. The record-setting game of kickball was 50 hours long and was played in Rowlett, Texas (USA). The game started on April 9 and didn't finish until the two teams of 20 players finished their 220th inning on April 11. Team Toomas and team Teteh were made up of players ranging from age 18 to 53. Players took just one three-hour break during the game. After the break, they continued playing another eight hours of kickball! The Toomas team won with a score of 286 runs to 216. The rules of kickball are similar to those of baseball. However, players roll and kick a larger, softer ball instead of throw and hit a ball with a bat.

● A kickball team is taking a break on the field. Use the clues to write the name of each player where it belongs.

	1	2	3	4	5
1					
2					
3					
4					
5					

1. Lee is in the same row as Mona but in the column just to the left.

2. Miguel is in an odd-numbered row but an even-numbered column. No other students are in his row or column.

3. Jackie is located two boxes diagonally above Lee.

4. Nicole is in the same row as Jackie but as far away as she can get.

5. Lee is not in the bottom row.

CD-104549

Thinking Young

Oldest Female in a Tandem Parachute Jump
September 30, 2004

Do you think you might jump out of an airplane when you are 100 years and 60 days old? Estrid Geertsen (Denmark) sure did. She was the oldest person to skydive along with an instructor. When a parachutist jumps with a more-experienced instructor, it is called "tandem jumping." Geertsen made this jump from 13,100 feet (4,000 m) off the ground over Roskilde, Denmark. Many people have tried to set world records in their later years. Geertsen made it into the Guinness World Records category of "Amazing Feats by Golden Oldies." It sure helped to have a zest for life and a love for jumping out of airplanes!

● **Use the clues to find the age of each person in the riddles.**

1. Beth is 4 times younger than Ava. Claire is 6 years younger than Beth. Ava is 10 times older than Claire.

   Ava: _____

   Beth: _____

   Claire: _____

2. Jake is 3 years old. Multiply his age by Simone's age to get Mom's age. Grandpa's age is Mom's age with the digits reversed. Only one person's age is an even number.

   Simone: _____

   Mom: _____

   Grandpa: _____

Walking Tall

Fastest Marathon on Stilts
April 13, 2008

● Stilts make legs appear longer. Extra letters make words longer. The underlined words in the following passage are too short. Each word is missing its first letter. Read the passage. Figure out what the underlined words should be. Write the missing letters in the spaces provided. The boxed letters, in order, will spell the nickname of this towering Guinness World Records record holder.

_____ _____ _____ _____ _____ _____ _____ _____   _____ _____ _____ _____ _____

Ma__r__athons are exciting __**vents**. Some people run to __**in**. Others run to improve their personal times. __**till**, others run to raise money for ch__a__rity. And, __**hen** there are those folks who run to set bizarre records. In 2008, more than 30,000 people participated in __**he** London marathon. Thirty people attempted to set new Gu__i__nness World Records records. Twelve were successful. One of these __**alented** record holders __**as** Michelle Frost (UK). She crossed the 26.2-mile (42.2-km) fi__n__ish line in 8 hours, 25 minutes. The fastest female runner had finished 6 __**ours** earlier! But, Frost was still ecstatic with the results. That's b__e__cause __**his** young scout leader was running on wooden stilts that were 4 feet (1.2 m) high! Frost set the record __**or** the Fastest (and possibly only) Marathon o__n __**tilts**. And, she also raised thousands of dollars for charity!

Frost's beaver scout troop had no trouble __**potting** her during the race. __**he** to__w__ered above all of the other racers an__d__ her nine-foot-__**all** legs were clothed in __**right** __**ants**. The rainy day m__a__de the roads slippery. __**round** mile 22, Frost fell. It's a long drop onto hard pa__v__ement __**hen** you're wearing stilts. But, Frost just climbed back up __**gain** and finish__e__d the __**ace**.

CD-104549

Most Soccer Ball Touches in 30 Seconds (Female)
February 23, 2008

How many times can you touch a soccer ball in 30 seconds without letting it hit the ground? Try bouncing the ball on the tip of your toe. Now try doing it really, really fast. Do you think you can do it as fast as Chloe Hegland (Canada)? She beat the 30-second record by touching the ball 163 times while keeping the ball in the air. She set that record in Madrid, Spain. But, she sets records closer to home too. Back in Canada, Hegland set the record for the Most Soccer Ball Touches in One Minute while keeping the ball in the air. She set that 339-touch record on November 3, 2007. Once she gets a groove going, there's no stopping Hegland!

● Hegland is setting records in a fraction of a minute. Solve the problems in the puzzle below to find more fractions. Fill in the blanks across and down.

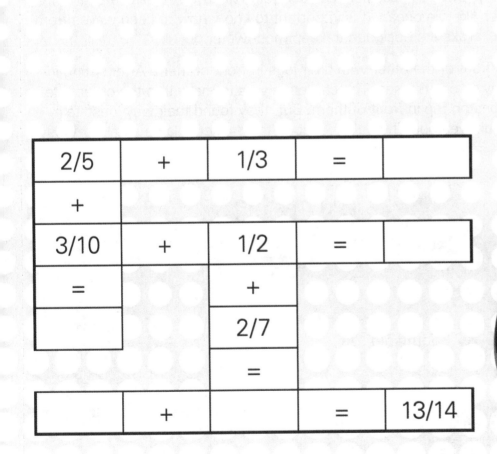

2/5	+	1/3	=	
+				
3/10	+	1/2	=	
=		+		
		2/7		
		=		
	+		=	13/14

CD-104549

Navigating Across the Sea

Fastest North Sea Crossing by Double Sea Kayak
July 4, 2009

In just 17 hours, 53 minutes, Simon Worsley and Ian Castro (both UK) crossed the North Sea to raise money for their favorite charity. They paddled from Southwold in the UK to Zeebrugge in Belgium. How did they do it? They worked together to set a record using a double kayak meant for sea travel. The two men share a previous record for the single sea kayak crossing of the North Sea.

Kayaking across a vast body of water such as the North Sea requires a lot of practice and good teamwork. Kayaking partners often begin training together on a pond or a lake. They practice paddling to learn how to keep their paddles from hitting each other. They also learn how to make turns together, which can be tricky. Once the partners can control their kayak in still water, it is time to practice in choppier water, like the ocean. It is important to know how to keep waves from crashing over the craft, although kayaks are designed to keep most water out.

Castro and Worsley sat one in front of the other with their legs in front of them. After sitting in the kayak, they were on their way across the sea. The challenge was to make it to the other side. They had an 87-mile (140-km) nonstop trip in front of them. But, they found their way, despite a very choppy sea and some difficult weather. Through sponsors, they raised a large sum of money for their charity.

● People can use plot points on maps to help them find their way. Use the grid below to help you answer the questions.

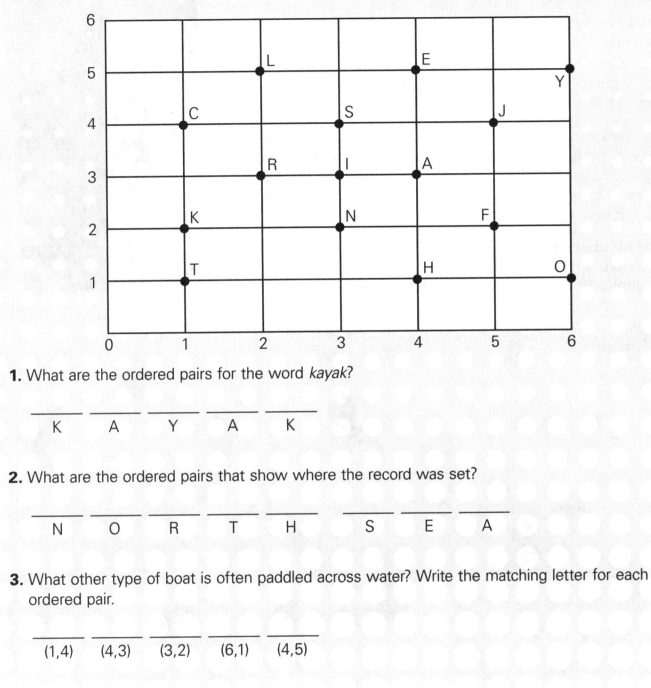

1. What are the ordered pairs for the word *kayak*?

K	A	Y	A	K

2. What are the ordered pairs that show where the record was set?

N	O	R	T	H	S	E	A

3. What other type of boat is often paddled across water? Write the matching letter for each ordered pair.

___	___	___	___	___
(1,4)	(4,3)	(3,2)	(6,1)	(4,5)

4. What do all kayakers wear to paddle around in ponds, lakes, or oceans? Write the matching letter for each ordered pair.

___	___	___	___		___	___	___	___	___	___
(2,5)	(3,3)	(5,2)	(4,5)		(5,4)	(4,3)	(1,4)	(1,2)	(4,5)	(1,1)

Spinboy Strikes Again!

Most Head Spins in One Minute
November 18, 2010

He has been called "Spinboy Aichi." So far, no one can compete with Aichi Ono's (Japan) number of spins on his head. His latest record was 135 amazing spins in one minute. He set the record as part of a televised celebration of Guinness World Records Day in Tokyo, Japan. It was Ono's fifth successful attempt to break the record in this category.

Ono gets himself ready with a few slow spins. After he gains some momentum, he spins on his head with his feet in the air. He gains more and more speed as he brings his feet and knees in toward himself. Soon, he is spinning like a top! You can get dizzy just from watching him!

● The numbers in these tops got mixed up. Unscramble each set of numbers and put them in order to make a multiplication problem. Use every number.

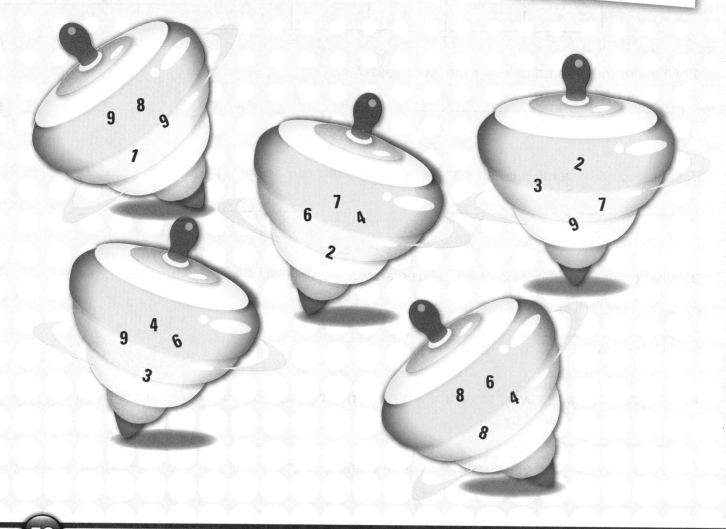

CD-104549

© Carson-Dellosa

Hoppity Hop

Fastest 100 Meters on a Space Hopper (Female)
September 26, 2004

In 2004, a group of Scottish mathematicians from the University of St. Andrews organized a fund-raiser. By the end of the day, they had raised a lot of money for charity. They had also set three new world records in space hopping! Only Dee McDougall's (UK) record for bouncing 328 feet (100 m) in 39.88 seconds still holds. When you play with a space hopper, you don't move any faster, farther, or higher than normal. But, as the mathematicians discovered, it is just fun! A space hopper is a big bouncy ball with handles. Some Americans call this toy a "hoppity hop." The Dutch call it a "skippybal." In Italy, it is simply called a "hop"! The inventor of this toy didn't actually call it any of those names.

● To find out what the inventor called this big bouncing ball, work the puzzle below. Beside each clue is a rhyming word. The rhyming words describe the action you perform to make this toy move. Use the clues to fill in the blanks. The boxed letters, in order, will spell the original name of this bouncing toy.

___ ___ ___ - ___ ___ ___

1. pump   ___ ___ ___ □

2. top   ___ □ ___

3. pounce   ___ ___ ___ □ ___ ___

4. heap   ___ ___ □ ___

5. sound   ___ □ ___ ___ ___

6. bring   ___ ___ ___ □ ___

CD-104549

Ping-Pong® Pals

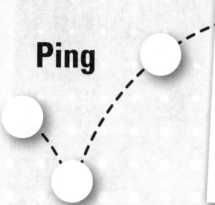

Longest Table Tennis Rally
August 14, 2004

Ping

Pong

On an August day in 2004, Brian and Steve Seibel (both USA) decided to play a little game of table tennis (also known as ping-pong) at their local YMCA. They grabbed a pair of paddles and a ball and started to play—and play and play! Their record-breaking ping-pong rally continued for 8 hours, 15 minutes, 1 second. Finally, one of them missed a shot. The record book tells how long the Seibels rallied, but it doesn't indicate who ended the rally. Considering the length of time they had been playing, they were probably both relieved!

● This sport is called table tennis because it is basically a tennis game played on a table. To the right is a labeled list of pieces of furniture (such as a table) that you might find in a house. Beside it is a list of sports. The words in both lists are missing their first letters. Write the missing letters. Then, match each furniture word to the sport that begins with the same first letter as that piece of furniture.

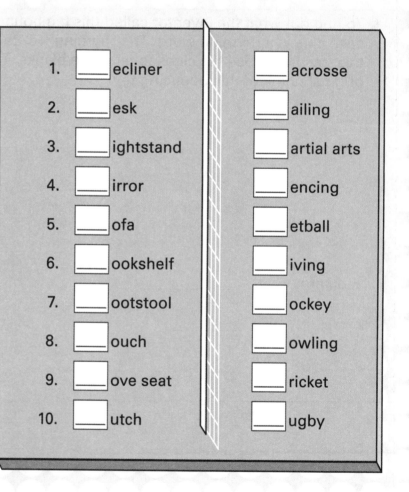

1. ____ecliner   ____acrosse
2. ____esk   ____ailing
3. ____ightstand   ____artial arts
4. ____irror   ____encing
5. ____ofa   ____etball
6. ____ookshelf   ____iving
7. ____ootstool   ____ockey
8. ____ouch   ____owling
9. ____ove seat   ____ricket
10. ____utch   ____ugby

A Balancing Act

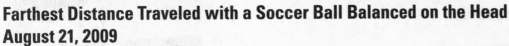

Farthest Distance Traveled with a Soccer Ball Balanced on the Head
August 21, 2009

Yee Ming Low (Malaysia) can do some amazing tricks with a soccer ball. He walked 6.915 miles (11.129 km) with a soccer ball balanced on his head. How long does it take someone to walk that far with a soccer ball on his head? It took Low 2 hours, 38 minutes, 44 seconds to get the job done. Low is no stranger to soccer either. He traveled 6,000 miles (9,656 km) from his home in Malaysia to play soccer for a college in the United Kingdom.

Low enjoys setting records for other soccer ball tricks as well. What's more, Low seems to enjoy walking with soccer balls on his head. He also holds the Guinness World Records record for the fastest mile (1.6 km) and the fastest 100 meters (328 feet) while balancing a soccer ball on his head.

● You can make a balancing act of balls too! In the space below, draw exactly 30 balls stacked into a pyramid. Start with a square base. Remember that you will be viewing your pyramid from above, not from the side. Use a different color for each layer of balls so that you do not get confused.

Wakeboarding Grandma

Oldest Competitive Wakeboarder
July 25, 2009

When Linda "Maw" Brown (USA) was born in 1945, no one had ever heard of wakeboarding. It wasn't until Brown was in her late 40s that this extreme sport was invented. Wakeboarding grew out of surfing, waterskiing, snowboarding, and skateboarding. The term *wake* refers to a water wave. A wakeboarder skims on top of the water while being pulled by a boat. It was only by chance that Brown started wakeboarding. She won a wakeboard at a charity event and decided to try it. She was already in her late 50s. To her shock, she loved it! "It just kind of came natural to me," she said. Since then, Brown has continued to wakeboard a couple of times every week. Brown's grandchildren convinced her to try for a Guinness World Records record. At a tournament in July 2009, Brown placed fifth out of more than 300 participants. Even though she didn't win, that event led Guinness World Records to recognize Brown as the Oldest Competitive Wakeboarder, female or male, in the world. Can you guess her age at the time? She was 63 years and 227 days old.

● Here is a list of Brown's record words. Beside it is a scrambled list of the opposites of these words. Unscramble the words. Then, write the correct number label beside the matching opposite word in Brown's column.

Brown's Record Words	Scrambled Opposites
ever ____	1. aefk ____ ____ ____ ____
late ____	2. aelry ____ ____ ____ ____ ____
more ____	3. bmoott ____ ____ ____ ____ ____ ____
natural ____	4. dehpsu ____ ____ ____ ____ ____ ____
oldest ____	5. eenrv ____ ____ ____ ____ ____
pulled ____	6. egnostuy ____ ____ ____ ____ ____ ____ ____
top ____	7. elos ____ ____ ____ ____
win ____	8. elss ____ ____ ____ ____

Bunny Hop

Highest Bicycle Bunny Hop
May 17, 2009

Most people think of bicycles as things that move forward. But, some people like to make their bikes hop in the air like bunnies! In a bunny hop, the bicyclist jumps with both wheels off the ground at the same time. During a competition, the bicyclist clears a bar set at a certain height. Benito Ros (Spain) set the record for the Highest Bicycle Bunny Hop. He hopped his bicycle 4 feet 8 inches (1.42 m) in the air. He set the record during a cycling competition. Ros and five other bicyclists qualified for the finals competition. Only Ros and two of the other bicyclists could reach the 1.42-meter mark. However, Ros was the only one who cleared the bar!

● Solve the problems. Then, use the key to find the answer to the riddle.

T = 3.736	I = 3.9192	O = 38.213	H = 2.8613
P = 2.9575	! = 8.1477	O = 1.088	T = 378.9

1. 8.45
    × .35

2. .340
    × 3.2

3. 9.23
    × .31

4. 5.68
    × .69

5. 421
    × .9

6. 8.23
    × .99

7. 7.21
    × 5.3

8. 4.67
    × .8

What did one bunny say to the other?

___ ___ ___   ___ ___   ___ ___ ___
 3   7   1   5   2   4   8   6

Car Surfing

Fastest Speed for a Surfboard Towed by a Car
February 2, 2007

What happens when a world champion kite surfer and a celebrity race car driver get together? They set a new Guinness World Records record of course! Watersport expert Stephanie Rowsell (UK) and stunt driver Ben Collins (UK) hold the record for the Fastest Speed for a Surfboard Towed by a Car. Surfer Rowsell sped along the surface of the water at a rate of 36 mph (57.93 km/h), while Collins drove along the beach towing her. Collins had to drive the car through shallow water to make sure that Rowsell had the water depth she needed to surf.

● Each sentence below describes how Rowsell and Collins planned ahead to make sure their record attempt was successful. Using the word bank, write the missing words.

1. The beach sand had to be _____ and flat.

2. The car had to drive through _____ water and sand.

3. Rowsell had to wear a GPS, or "global positioning system," unit to record her _____.

4. The "fins" on the bottom of the surfboard had to be _____ than normal to keep Rowsell from getting stuck in the _____.

5. The _____ had to be low so that the beach was fully exposed.

6. Collins had to accelerate very quickly so that the _____ would not tip _____.

7. Collins had to drive _____ so that Rowsell wouldn't be _____ off the surfboard.

8. Collins had to maintain his speed through the shallow _____ so that the surfboard wouldn't _____.

Word Bank

carefully
hard
knocked
over
salt
sand
sink
smaller
speed
surfboard
tide
water

Hats Off to You!

Fastest Time to Score a Hat Trick in Women's Ice Hockey
March 4, 2006

In sports, a *hat trick* is when a single player scores three times in a single game. Melissa Horvat (Canada) scored an ice hockey hat trick in just 35 seconds! Her team, Burlington 1 Bantams, was playing Stoney Creek in Ontario, Canada, in a play-off game. Horvat scored all three of her goals in the third period of the game. She made the goals with 8.56, 8.48, and 8.21 minutes left on the clock.

The exact reason for the name *hat trick* is unknown. Some people say it is because people throw their hats onto the field when the feat is accomplished. Others say that players used to be given free hats when they performed their feats. What we do know is that many players go their whole careers without scoring a hat trick!

● Three times is the magic number for a hat trick. For each shape below, draw exactly 3 lines to create 4 triangles of equal size.

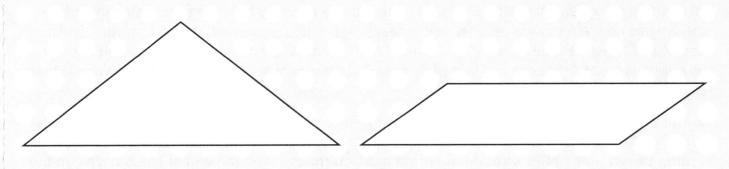

● Now, draw exactly 3 lines to divide the shapes below into 4 triangles of equal size.

CD-104549

Off-Road Biking

Longest Tightrope Crossing by Bicycle
October 15, 2008

Some kids want to grow up to be like their parents. They want to have the same type of job or work in the same business. This wasn't the case for Nik Wallenda (USA). He comes from a family of circus performers. The Flying Wallendas have been entertaining audiences for more than 200 years. Although Nik Wallenda first performed as a clown at the age of two, he wanted to become a circus veterinarian. But, his talent and family history persuaded him to join the family business.

In 2008, Wallenda set the record for the Longest Tightrope Crossing by Bicycle. On live TV, Wallenda biked across a tightrope for a distance of 235 feet (71.63 m). That's two-thirds the length of a football field! The "bike path" he followed was a thin wire strung tightly between two buildings. Wallenda didn't wear a safety harness. He had no safety net. All he had was a balancing pole in his hands. And, he was more than 13 stories in the air! Wallenda used a regular bike with the tires and handlebars removed. He rode by carefully balancing the metal rims of the wheels on the narrow wire. Just before reaching the end of his ride, the bike started to slide backward. "It was a little bit hairy for a minute there," said Wallenda. But, he recovered and set a new world record. Wallenda is a true performer. "My family history and my family tradition is that the show must go on."

● The high wire on the next page is coated in letters. Above the wire are five bicycle wheels. Each wheel contains a single vowel. Imagine that you are moving each wheel one at a time slowly across the wire. What words can you make when the wheel stops between the letters? For each vowel, write those words in the spaces provided. Words created using just the first two letters on the wire ("n" and "t") have been filled in for you.

CD-104549

m n t g h (t) f l y n g t (h) n s t r n g (r) m s w t h f r s l (w)(i) b j s t s t p p t h (o) l d n d s t n w (s) h w m (s) t

a	e	i	o	u
an	men	in	on	nut
at		it	no	
			not	
			to	

● Write the circled letters from the wire, in order, on the blank lines to spell the fancy word that means "tightrope walker."

___ u ___ a ___ ___ u ___ i ___ ___

CD-104549

That's Pedal Power!

Greatest Distance by Pedal-Powered Boat in 24 Hours
May 7, 2005

Most people take pedal-powered boats on a lake to relax. The boats are perfect for watching wildlife and enjoying a bright summer day. But, the Trieste Waterbike Team (Italy) has a pedal-powered boat that is meant for high-speed travel. The team pedaled nonstop for 24 hours and traveled 110.2 miles (177.3 km) to set a Guinness World Records record. The team did the whole journey without changing their three-member crew. Their vehicle looked like half bike and half boat! The Trieste Waterbike Team enters (and wins) many competitions in water biking.

● A water biking team of four did some math problems. But, who did which problem? Solve the problems below. Then, use the clues to find out which team member came up with which answer.

1. 783
    × 46

2. 889
    × 80

3. 7,883 ÷ 6 =

4. 3,276 ÷ 7 =

- Colby has a three-digit answer.

- Macon's answer is not a whole number.

- Logan's answer has three odd numbers.

- Abe's answer has three even numbers.

Colby's answer is _____.

Macon's answer is _____.

Logan's answer is _____.

Abe's answer is _____.

Can Cracker

Most Soft Drink Cans Broken with a Whip in Three Minutes
April 11, 2009

Adam "Crack" Winrich (USA) holds seven world records in whip cracking. In 2009, Winrich was a guest on the set of *Lo Show dei Record* in Italy. The producers hoped he would perform his most recent record-setting whip trick of putting out 50 candles in one minute. But, another guest was also performing a trick with candles. The producers decided they wanted something totally new. "Crack" told them he could slice a soft drink can in half with one flip of the whip. Three minutes later, 23 cans were cut in half, and Winrich's seventh Guinness World Records record was official. Winrich considers this to be the perfect trick if he can still manage to drink the standing half cans of soda afterward!

● Fill in the soft drink cans with the matching letters from the words in the word bank. The soft drink can groups contain words the same length as the word bank words. Be careful! Some words have the same number of letters, but only one sentence will make sense.

Word Bank				
after	and	became	Crack	Crusade
in	Indiana	interested	Jones	Last
movie	seeing	the	the	whips

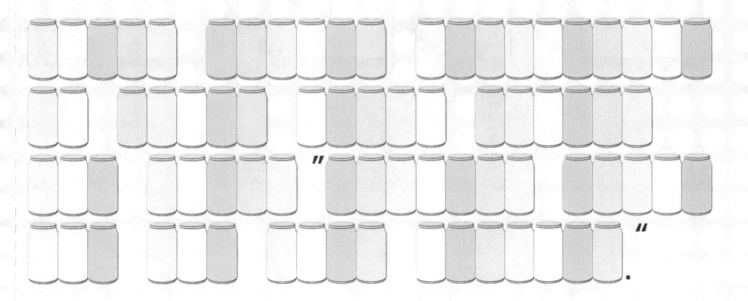

Elbow Room, Please!

Three Contortionists in a Box (Longest Duration)
September 20, 2009

Contortionists are entertainers who twist and bend their bodies into unnatural positions. Skye Broberg, Nele Siezen, and Jola Siezen (all New Zealand) are contortionists who work as performers and try to entertain audiences. To break the world record, the three of them climbed into a box measuring 26 x 27 x 22 inches (66 x 68 x 55 cm). If that's not difficult enough, they stayed inside the box for 6 minutes, 13.5 seconds! That's a tight squeeze!

● To find the volume of the box the contortionists got into, find the product of the box's height, width, and length. Compare that volume with the volume of the boxes below. Put the boxes in order from least volume to greatest volume.

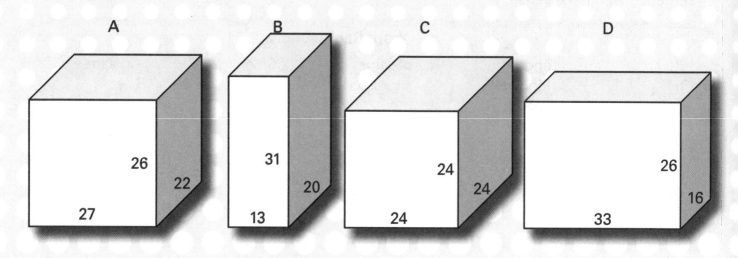

A — 26, 22, 27

B — 31, 20, 13

C — 24, 24, 24

D — 26, 16, 33

Volume from least to greatest:

box _____

box _____

box _____

box _____

CD-104549

Bouncing Bungee Jumping

Most Indoor Bungee Jumps in 24 Hours
November 5–6, 2007

You can do much more than just shop at the West Edmonton Mall. You can bungee jump too! In 2006, teenager Peter Charney (Canada) bungee jumped over a pool a total of 106 times in 24 hours. His bungee jumping raised money for charity. In 2007, Peter was back again. This time, he managed more than twice that number of jumps. "I remember reading the Guinness [World Records] book since 1997," said Peter. "I've always wanted to be in [it]." With his incredible 225 jumps, Peter achieved his goal: a world record for the Most Indoor Bungee Jumps in 24 Hours.

● Modern bungee jumpers attach long elastic cords to their bodies when they jump. The jumper bounces upside down in midair, and the cord snaps up and down. The idea behind bungee jumping comes from an ancient Pacific island ritual. Instead of elastic cords, the Bunlap people used tree vines.

Start with the word *LAND*. Change exactly one letter at a time to create a new word. The boxes indicate the letters to change. Continue changing one letter in each new word until all of the words have been completed. All of the new words must be real words. (Hint: the new letters, in some order, are *D, E, V,* and *I.*)

The first and last words, put together, form the original phrase for *bungee jump*.

LAND ___ ___ ___ ___

1. LAND

2. ___ ___ ___ [ ]

3. ___ [ ] ___ ___

4. ___ ___ [ ] ___

5. [ ] ___ ___ ___

Largest Skateboard
February 25, 2009

Giants should be able to skateboard too, right? At least that is what Rob Dyrdek and Joe Ciaglia (both USA) must have been thinking when they set the record for building the world's Largest Skateboard. They unveiled their creation on the MTV series called *Rob Dyrdek's Fantasy Factory*. On the show, Dyrdek tries to set various world records. The show also features a huge indoor skateboard park. The world record skateboard has the following dimensions:

- Length: 36 feet 7 inches (11.14 m)

- Width: 8 feet 8 inches (2.63 m)

- Height: 3 feet 7.5 inches (1.10 m)

● The length of this mega skateboard is 36 feet 7 inches (11.14 m). Suppose you wanted to keep doubling the length of the skateboard. Draw a line to connect the 36-foot-7-inch board to the one that is double in length. Double the length each time you draw a connecting line.

Faster Than a Fish

Fastest 100-Meter Hurdles Wearing Swim Fins (Female)
December 8, 2010

You may have seen people run 100-meter dashes in which the runners leap over hurdles in their paths. But, have you ever seen it done while the runner is wearing swim fins? It may be a comic sight, but think about it. Veronica Torr (New Zealand) actually ran 328 feet (100 m) while jumping 10 hurdles and wearing swim fins. And, she did it in 18.523 seconds, beating her 2009 record of 19.278 seconds. It took less than one second to set a new record. This heptathlon athlete practices all sorts of events. She does hurdles, long jumps, high jumps, and sprints. She also does shot put, javelin throws, and 800-meter (2,624.7-foot) runs. It's all in a day's work. So, why not put on some swim fins and conquer a new sport that hasn't quite been invented yet—swim fin hurdles!

● To jump over a hurdle, all you need is a solid figure. Which figure below do you think cannot be folded to make a solid? _____

To see if you are right, trace the shapes onto another sheet of paper. Then, cut and fold.

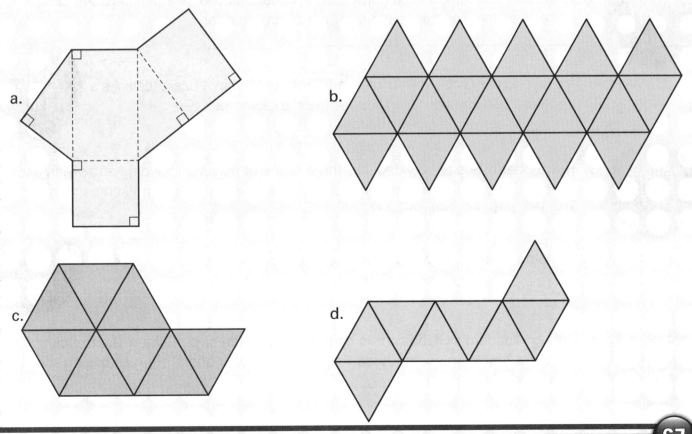

a.

b.

c.

d.

CD-104549

Globetrotter Gal

First Woman to Play with the Harlem Globetrotters
1985

In 1985, Olympic basketball player Lynette Woodard (USA) became the first woman ever to play with the Harlem Globetrotters. The Globetrotters combine fantastic basketball with hilarious entertainment. Dribbles and dunks are part of the Globetrotters' game, but so are clowns and comedians. Woodard played with the team for two years. She left to play professional ball in Italy and Japan. Woodard finished her basketball career with the WNBA (Women's National Basketball Association) just as it was starting up. Today she's a stockbroker. But, Woodard still loves to play basketball. "The opportunities [for me] were there at the right time. You prepare, you work hard at it, you practice," says Woodard. "You shoot your best shot."

● **Below are five basketballs. Each has an associated question. The basketballs contain the scrambled answers. Unscramble the answers and write them on the lines.**

a b
c k l l
o s

1. What was the name of the game that Woodard played as a girl by rolling up a piece of clothing and shooting it off her bedroom door?

___ ___ ___ ___ ___ ___ ___ ___

2. Woodard's cousin, also a Globetrotter, showed her how to spin a basketball. As a child, what did Woodard consider the Globetrotters' tricks to be?

___ ___ ___ ___ ___

a c g
i m

3. The Globetrotters are divided into three types of players, including showmen and dribblers. Woodard was the third type—a player who jumps and scores. What was this type of player called? ___ ___ ___ ___ ___ ___

e h o p
p r

4. To play for the Globetrotters, how did Woodard's basketball skills have to appear?

___ ___ ___ ___ ___ ___

e i l m
p s

5. During Woodard's Globetrotters career, a young fan said, "When she dribbles, it's like she's bouncing one of these through a revolving door." He was talking about what kind of vegetable? ___ ___ ___ ___ ___ ___

a o o p
t t

A Swim in the Amazon

Longest Journey Swimming
April 8, 2007

It takes a strong swimmer to swim the entire length of the 3,300-mile-long (5,310.8-km) Amazon River in just 67 days. Martin Strel (Slovenia) is definitely the man to do it. He started his journey in Atalaya, Peru. He finished in Belém, Brazil, a whole other country away. It took Strel from February 1 to April 8 to get the job done. The Amazon can be a tricky and dangerous river. This made some days better for swimming than others. After all, the water was filled with parasites and piranhas! Some days, Strel swam as little as 5.5 miles (9 km). Other days, he swam as

many as 78.9 miles (127 km). Strel has been a professional marathon swimmer for more than 30 years. Over the past 10 years, he has been setting his sights on swimming in rivers, lakes, and oceans around the world.

● The Amazon piranha has four routes that will take him from the beginning of his swim and get him back home. Each route adds up to 1,700 miles. Find the missing distance for each route so that the piranha makes it back to his home. You must start in the middle and touch five boxes as you go. The third box will always be blank. The fifth number must lead you back to the center. Fill in the distance for each missing box.

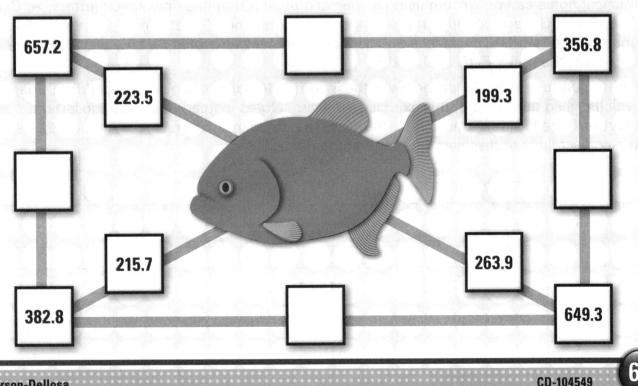

Morning Exercises

Largest Multi-Venue Dance Class
July 11, 2008

You don't have to go to dance classes to be able to dance at school. Just ask 26,797 students in Liverpool (UK). That's how many kids took part in the SportsLinx™ 2008 health and fitness program. For a year and a half, students at primary schools across the city practiced dance steps for 10 minutes every morning. During the grand performance, a local radio station played the dance music for everyone to hear. With 124 schools participating, this dance workshop set a world record as the Largest Multi-Venue Dance Class ever. Dancing burns calories and is fun as well. What a great way to start a school day!

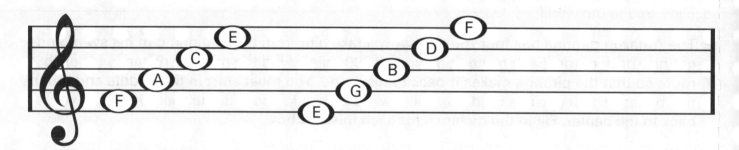

- Musical notes can be written using a special alphabet that has only seven letters: *A, B, C, D, E, F,* and *G.* Each sound is represented by a round "note" that can be written on lines or spaces on a "staff." The spaces on this staff represent the notes *F, A, C,* and *E.* The lines represent the notes *E, G, B, D,* and *F.*

Written on the musical staff below is the incomplete name of one of the children's dances, which is also the name of this exercise program. Notes instead of alphabetic letters represent the letters *A* through *G.* Translate the notes into letters and write the letters on the correct lines to discover the name of the dance.

r i s___   ___ n ___   s h i n___   ___ ___ n ___ ___

A "Rally, Rally" Long Time

Longest Tennis Rally
August 9, 2008

A tennis rally can be fun to watch. But, when it lasts for 14 hours, 31 minutes, it goes beyond fun and becomes amazing. The Longest Tennis Rally was between Ettore Rossetti and Angelo A. Rossetti (both USA). The event happened at a tennis club in North Haven, Connecticut. It took the twin brothers 25,944 strokes to set their record. The two tennis teachers doubled their previous best rally, which was also a record. But, this time they finally beat the world record by 1,248 strokes. And, there are no hard feelings between the twins because of one of them missing the final ball. The men just simply stopped playing at 12:01 A.M. on August 10 to stop the rally! Good game!

● The Rossetti twins hit the ball 100 percent of the time! Solve each percent problem and use the key to write the word that shows the audience's reaction to the Rossetti twins.

A = 100	L = 20	T = 15	Y = 8	H = 25	R = 3	W = 4

1. 20% of 20	6. 15% of 20
2. 25% of 100	7. 20% of 500
3. 50% of 200	8. 40% of 50
4. 30% of 50	9. 20% of 100
5. 100% of 100	10. 40% of 20

___ ___ ___ ___   ___   ___ ___ ___ ___ ___!
 1   2   3   4   5   6   7   8   9   10

High-Speed Sledding

Fastest Speed Riding a Zipflbob®
April 11, 2009

Is it a bird? Is it a plane? It's neither! It's student Frederik Eiter (Austria) on his Zipflbob! In 2009, Eiter zoomed down the Pitztal Glacier at a record speed of 97.6 miles (157 km) per hour. A Zipflbob is a high-speed sled. It was invented in the 1970s and is especially popular in Europe. Zipflbobbers are hoping their extreme sledding sport will eventually become an Olympic event.

- The current winter Olympic sports are listed in the word bank below. Fill in the blanks with the correct sport. The boxed letters, in order, will spell the motto of the International Zipflbob Federation (IZF).

Word Bank

Alpine skiing	figure skating	short track speed skating
biathlon	freestyle skiing	skeleton
bobsleigh	ice hockey	ski jumping
cross-country skiing	luge	snowboarding
curling	Nordic combined	speed skating

Olympic Sports

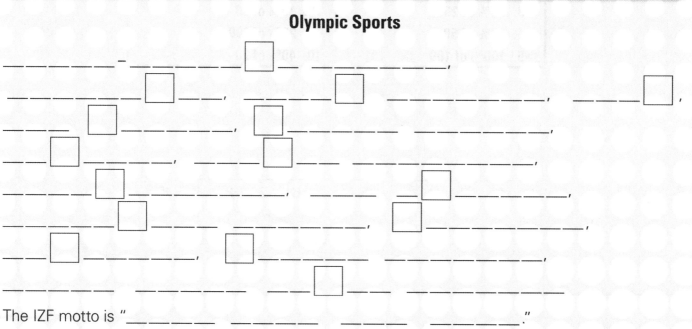

The IZF motto is "___ ___ ___ ___."

Ultimate Team Player

Most Sacrifice Bunts in a Baseball Career
August 2003

When someone is called a "team player," it is because that person does things that are for the good of the whole team and not just for his own glory. It is rare to see someone who is as much a team player as Masahiro Kawai (Japan). This professional baseball player made 514 sacrifice bunts during his 20-year career playing for the Yomiuri Giants. Also known as a sacrifice hit, a bunt is a small and gentle hit. It allows a base runner to advance to the next base while the other team scrambles for the ball. The bunter will most likely be called "out." At the same time, the other player gets a better chance at a run. The bunter gives up his turn for the team's chance of doing better. Between 1984 and 2003, Kawai was always ready to "take one for the team"!

● Each little calculation below is a bunt that adds up for the team. Fill in each calculation in the pyramid. Start from the bottom. Add each pair of numbers next to each other. Write the answer in the box just above the number pair. Move to the next row as you complete each row.

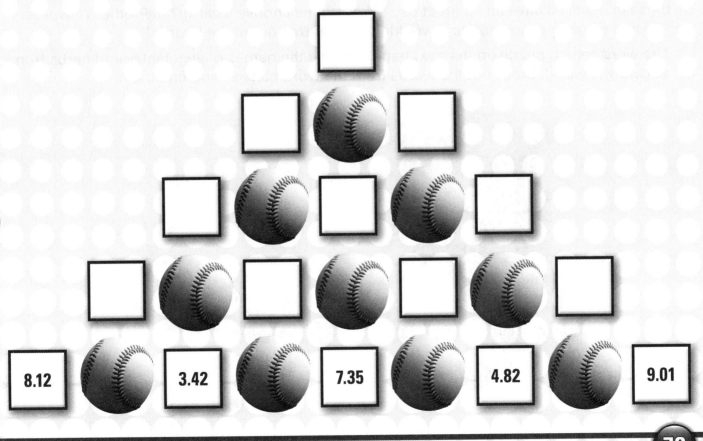

8.12   3.42   7.35   4.82   9.01

Catch That Carrot!

Fastest Marathon Dressed as a Vegetable
April 26, 2009

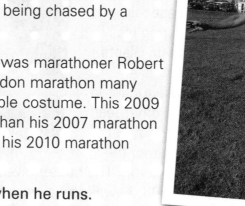

In 2009, a carrot crossed the Flora London Marathon finish line in just 3 hours, 34 minutes, 55 seconds. It smashed the previous Guinness World Records record for Fastest Vegetable. The carrot came in 90 minutes behind the first-place finisher. However, it finished one hour ahead of the average marathon participant. And, the carrot wasn't even being chased by a hungry rabbit!

The runner inside the carrot costume was marathoner Robert Prothero (UK). Prothero has run the London marathon many times. This was his first run in a vegetable costume. This 2009 carrot run was only 13 minutes slower than his 2007 marathon finish. But, it was 8 minutes faster than his 2010 marathon finish!

● Prothero raises money for charity when he runs. He thinks people are more likely to donate if he is in costume. Prothero's carrot run raised thousands of dollars for an organization that helps provide clean drinking water to some of the world's poorest people. "We all need safe, clean water to survive," says Prothero. "If I can provide a laugh for the supporters around the course, come away with a world record, and raise money to help those in need, I'll have had a great day." Why did he choose a carrot? In Prothero's words, "If I had run as a couch potato, I wouldn't have gotten out of the house!"

The word search puzzle on the next page contains the names of vegetables and herbs from all over the world. Cross out the words from the word bank as you find them.

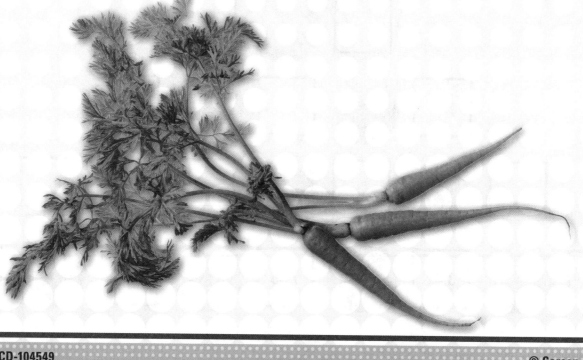

Word Bank

artichoke	cabbage	horseradish	rhubarb
avocado	cauliflower	leek	rutabaga
bamboo shoot	celery	mustard (greens)	squash
basil	corn	okra	Swiss chard
beans	endive	onion	turnip
bean sprout	fennel	parsnip	watercress
beet	fiddlehead	potato	yam
broccoli	gourd	pumpkin	zucchini

```
a  r  t  i  c  h  o  k  e  n  d  i  v  e  z
v  w  c  p  c  o  b  r  o  c  c  o  l  i  u
o  s  a  o  e  r  b  r  h  u  b  a  r  b  c
c  q  b  t  l  s  t  o  m  y  a  m  u  g  c
a  u  b  a  e  e  b  u  t  u  t  h  t  o  h
d  a  a  t  r  r  o  e  r  u  s  e  a  u  i
o  s  g  o  y  a  c  k  o  n  e  t  b  r  n
p  h  e  n  c  d  c  r  r  b  i  a  a  d  i
u  b  f  i  o  i  p  r  e  a  r  p  g  r  o
m  a  e  o  r  s  w  i  s  s  c  h  a  r  d
p  s  n  n  n  h  t  p  a  r  s  n  i  p  l
k  i  n  a  f  i  d  d  l  e  h  e  a  d  e
i  l  e  c  a  u  l  i  f  l  o  w  e  r  e
n  b  l  b  a  m  b  o  o  s  h  o  o  t  k
```

The unused letters, in order from top to bottom and left to right, will spell Prothero's 2009 marathon nickname.

___ __ ____   ___ ___ ___   __ __ _ __ __ __

CD-104549

Cycling by Hand

Farthest Distance by Hand-Cranked Cycle in 24 Hours (Male)
February 14–15, 2009

A hand-cranked cycle on the road always seems to turn a lot of heads. It's an interesting sight to see. But, the bikes are not strange to Thomas Lange (Germany). Lange set a record for the greatest distance covered by a hand-cranked cycle in 24 hours. He traveled 403.8 miles (649.85 km). He set the record during a cycling event in Sebring, Florida. The event started on February 14, 2009. Lange finished his journey the next day. A hand-cranked bicycle looks and operates very differently from a traditional bicycle. The low bike has two wheels in the back and one in the front. The cyclist lies on his back and cranks the bike with his hands while his feet stay put.

● The cyclists below are riding on a path around a stadium. The path is 2.3 miles around. Use the clues to figure out which cyclists came in first, second, and third place in the 2-hour race. Round each answer to the nearest hundredth of a mile and write it in the trophy.

- Jaden traveled a quarter of the distance Ebony traveled, plus twice the distance Dante traveled.

- Ebony traveled half the amount that Dante traveled, plus 20 1/2 miles.

- Dante traveled 13 1/4 times around the stadium.

_____ traveled the farthest distance in 2 hours.

CD-104549

Skateboarding Trip of a Lifetime

Longest Journey by Skateboard
August 28, 2008

Who else can claim that they skateboarded from Switzerland to China in a year and three months? Rob Thomson (New Zealand) went on a 7,555-mile (12,159-km) journey by skateboard. It was the trip of a lifetime! Thomson started his journey in Leysin, Switzerland, on June 24, 2007. He traveled through Germany, Belgium, the Netherlands, and England. On August 4, 2007, he took a sailboat across the Atlantic Ocean to Florida. This journey across the Atlantic took until December 7! He then skateboarded more than 3,435 miles (5,529 km) across the southern United States to California. But, the journey didn't stop there! He traveled to China and skateboarded 3,394 miles (5,462 km) on national highways from Xinjiang Province to Shanghai. During his trip, he experienced freezing temperatures. He recorded and wrote about his trip along the way. Now *that's* a long, interesting journey.

● Find the path the skateboarder below took from Florida to California. Connect the dots to show the multiples of 7.

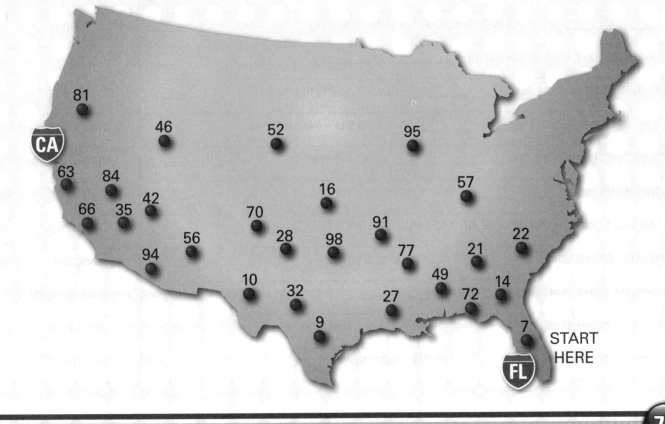

CD-104549

Camel Coming Through

Fastest 10K Run by Two People Wearing a Costume
December 3, 2006

Stuart Maycock and Shaun Marsden (both UK) are runners. Sometimes, they race alone. Sometimes, they race together in a relay. But, in the Percy Pud 10K (6.2-mile) race in 2006, Maycock and Marsden ran a little closer than usual. They crossed the finish line together, placing 96th and 97th among 1,130 competitors. That is not bad for two guys running in a camel suit! Their time was 40 minutes, 18 seconds, which was only 8 minutes behind the winner. Maycock and Marsden's camel costume was made for two people. Two distinct brains operated two sets of feet. A real camel could have run this same race in half the time and would have taken home first place!

● Each clue below relates to a word within one of the numbered animal names. Match the clues with the animals by writing the animal number beside the correct clue. Be careful! The clues will only help you figure out **one part** of the animal word.

Clues		Animals
Just because I <u>came</u> today, doesn't mean I will come tomorrow too.	_1_	1. <u>cam</u>el
I ___ ___ ___ all of the way to school, but I was still late.	___	2. butterfly
People who have a lot of money are ___ ___ ___ ___.	___	3. crane
Neil Armstrong was the first ___ ___ ___ to walk on the moon.	___	4. hedgehog
My sister's favorite class is ___ ___ ___ because she loves to draw.	___	5. hippopotamus
The bike path runs along the ___ ___ ___ ___ of the road.	___	6. octopus
Is that water in the ___ ___ ___ boiling yet?	___	7. ostrich
All of those apple cores I dumped into the garden are going to ___ ___ ___.	___	8. parrot
She said I had to use a ___ ___ ___ instead of a pencil.	___	9. penguin
They were going to drive to the concert, ___ ___ ___ the car wouldn't start.	___	10. salamander
Write your name at the ___ ___ ___ of your test paper.	___	11. wallaby
Are you going to eat ___ ___ ___ of that macaroni?	___	12. warthog

CD-104549

Largest Soccer Ball
July 5, 2010

The world's Largest Soccer Ball is just too large to kick. It has a diameter of 51 feet 4 inches (15.66 m). KIA™ Motors and Emperor's Palace Resort and Casino created the ball in Johannesburg, South Africa. The ball is an exact replica of a World Cup ball from Mexico used in 1970. It has 32 separate panels and required more than 4,921 feet (1,500 m) of material to make. Twenty ropes held the ball in place so that it wouldn't roll. The ball took three-and-a-half hours to inflate and weighed in at 1,433 pounds (650 kg)! Emperor's Palace Resort displayed the ball for three weeks. The previous record for the Largest Soccer Ball was set in 2007 in Sudan. But, this new record is really quite extraordinary.

● Making a giant replica of a soccer ball takes a lot of calculations. Solve the problems in the puzzle below and figure out each missing calculation.

$3\frac{1}{2}$	×		=	$16\frac{1}{3}$
×				
	×	$2\frac{1}{2}$	=	3
=				
	×	$1\frac{1}{3}$	=	$5\frac{9}{15}$

Up and Over the Bar

Most Consecutive Gymnastic High Bar Giants
July 21, 2009

Have people ever told you that your "bar is set too high"? What they really mean is that they don't think you can achieve your goal. David Fahradyan (Armenia) sets his bar high—the gymnastics bar, that is. This gymnastics instructor can spin on the high bar over and over again, doing what are called "high bar giants." He holds on with his hands and completely stretches out his arms and legs during his spins. In 2005, Fahradyan made it into a book about Armenian heroes for these high bar giants. Then, he set the bar even higher, aiming for a Guinness World Records record. Fahradyan reached his new goal in 2009 when, in a little more than 10 minutes, he spun 350 dizzying high bar rotations. Now, Fahradyan is not only an expert in high bar giants, but he actually *is* a high bar giant!

Definitions	
_____	a law exam
_____	something longer than it is wide
_____	a pole
_____	except
_____	to block
_____	to lock

● The word *bar* looks simple, but it has many different meanings. Each sentence below uses *bar* in a unique way. Use words from the word bank to fill in the blanks. Match the sentences with the definitions by writing the sentence letter label beside the definition. Those letter labels, in order, will spell the people to whom Fahradyan dedicated his world record.

Word Bank

break	come	crossing	door	flood	lawyer
candy	cousin	dinner	everyone	grab	monkey

Sentences

I. Absolutely _____ is welcome to _____ to the party, **bar** none.

L. The _____ will **bar** people from _____ the bridge.

M. I can _____ onto that **bar** and swing like a _____ .

F. If my _____ passes her **bar** exam, she will become a _____ .

A. You won't want any _____ if you eat that _____ **bar** now.

Y. You had better **bar** the _____ in case someone tries to _____ into the house.

For the Love of the Sport

Most Wins of the IGSA Women's Downhill Skateboard Championships 2010

Brianne Davies (Canada) is an electrician who loves to cook. She also happens to be the winner of the 2008, 2009, and 2010 individual IGSA Women's Downhill Skateboard Championships. IGSA stands for International Gravity Sports Association. Gravity helps propel Davies and her skateboard down long, winding roads. Downhill skateboarding, also called "longboarding," is a tough sport. Crashes are common. "You just need to get back up and get rolling again," says Davies. But, even this champion knows her limits. At the end of 2010, Davies officially retired from competitive longboarding. She is looking forward to skateboarding for the love of the sport instead of trying to set records.

● Below are longboards of varied lengths. Each set of lines can hold a different word that can be found scrambled within the word *LONGBOARDING*. Write as many words as possible. Do not use any variations of the words *long* or *board*.

That's a Big Reach!

Farthest Dyno Move in Wall Climbing (Male)
June 14, 2009

When wall climbing, some handholds can be very far away and difficult for a climber to reach. When a climber launches from one set of handholds directly to a higher set, it is called a "dyno move." That's short for "dynamic move." Nicky de Leeuw (Holland) made one dynamic move on June 14, 2009. He reached 9 feet 2 inches (2.80 m) to make the world's Farthest Dyno Move in Wall Climbing for a Male. De Leeuw set the record at a World Cup event in Eindhoven, Holland. He made the move successfully on his second attempt. That's a good thing, because more than 150 people were watching him. Now that's an experienced wall climber! Since he started climbing in 1995, de Leeuw has found himself in some tricky climbing situations. It's a good thing he is so good at dyno moves!

● Each dyno move is a strategic move. Look at the climbing ropes below. They form Roman numerals. Move one rope in each problem to make the problem true. (Hint: You may move *any* rope you see.)

1. X + VII = XV

2. IX – VI = V

3. XVI – III = XI

4. V + XIII = XVI

Golden X-cellence

Youngest X Games Gold Medalist (Female)
August 7, 2004

At 14, Lyn-z Adams Hawkins (USA) became the Youngest X Games Gold Medalist (Female). She won her first gold in the Skateboard Vert competition in 2004. But, that was only the beginning. By the end of 2010, she had accumulated eight X Games medals, three of which are gold. Who knows how many more medals Lyn-z will earn?

Lyn-z received her first skateboard when she was two. But, her interest in skateboarding really started when her brother treated her to a membership at a club with a skate park. Lyn-z also surfs, snowboards, rides a dirt bike, and plays soccer. She even has her own character in a popular skateboarding video game. But, she doesn't even play it! As a world-class skateboarder, Lyn-z has become a role model for many young skaters. "Growing up, I wanted to be like my brother," she says. "But today, maybe other young girls will want to be like me."

● Skateboarders have invented all sorts of words to describe the different moves in their sport. Below are some of these words, but they are written in a secret alphabet-order code. Use the first answer to help you discover the code. Write your answers on the lines. The boxed letters, in order from left to right and top to bottom, will spell the skateboarding name of Lyn-z's video game character.

___ ___ ___ ___ ___ ___

ranp	IyPseop	Ywxwhhanewh
v e r t	__ __ __ __ [ ] __	__ __ __ __ __ __ __ __
jkhhea	**dwhb lela**	**ckkbu bkkp**
__ __ __ __ __	[ ] __ __ __ – __ __ __	__ __ __ __ __ __ __ __
bwgea	**ohwllu**	**jkoacnejz**
__ __ __ __	__ __ __ __ __ __	__ __ __ __ __ [ ] __ __
khhea	**pweh oheza**	**bqjxkt**
__ __ __ [ ]	__ __ __ __ __ __ __ [ ] __	__ __ __ __ __

Just Skipping Along

Farthest Distance Skipping on a Rolling Globe
June 28, 2003

People set records in all kinds of places. Katya Davidson (USA) set a world record at a community parade. She traveled a distance of 2,008 feet 4 inches (612.13 m) while skipping on a rolling globe at the parade. That's quite a distance! The globe itself was 24 inches (60 cm) high. The event that Davidson was celebrating was the Red, White & Blue Parade in Citrus Heights, California. The games were known as the Skipping Games. Davidson certainly had something to celebrate—namely a great sense of balance!

● The numbers in these globes got mixed up. Unscramble each set of numbers and put them in order to make a division problem. Use every number.

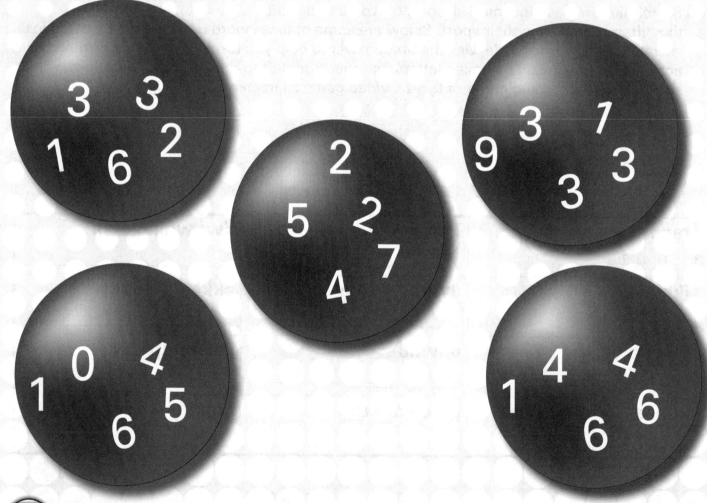

Largest Ice-Skating Pinwheel
September 7, 2008

The largest human pinwheel doesn't spin in the wind. It spins on ice. In 2008, a group of 65 talented skaters from the *Holiday on Ice* show joined to create the Largest Ice-Skating Pinwheel in the world. Because of the size of the wheel, a special square-shaped outdoor rink had to be made in Germany for the record attempt. The "wheel" is actually a difficult skating routine. It looks like a big line of skaters rotating around a single point. The trickiest part of the routine is forming the wheel. The line starts from the center and builds outward on both sides. The skaters close to the middle must move slowly so that the later skaters can catch up. The farther along the wheel a skater is, the faster he would have to skate to join the end of the pinwheel.

● Below are seven word puzzles. Each puzzle contains three words. The words are one, three, and five letters long. For each word, add one letter on both ends to create the next word. The letters used in each puzzle are listed alphabetically within the box.

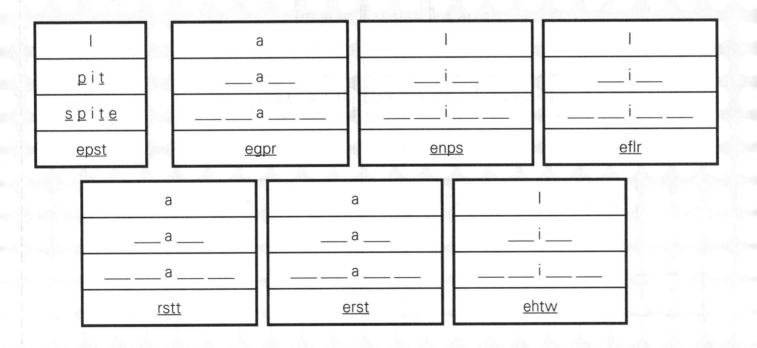

I	a	I	I
p i t	__ a __	__ i __	__ i __
s p i t e	__ __ a __ __	__ __ i __ __	__ __ i __ __
epst	egpr	enps	eflr

a	a	I
__ a __	__ a __	__ i __
__ __ a __ __	__ __ a __ __	__ __ i __ __
rstt	erst	ehtw

What a Team!

Fastest 100-Mile Relay by a Team of 10
December 31, 2009

The fastest time to complete 100 miles (170 km) by a team of 10 in a relay is 8 hours, 19 minutes, 53 seconds. The 10-man team was part of a cross-country running club from Ada, Oklahoma (USA). The team set the record on New Year's Eve in freezing temperatures and even braved windy conditions and a bit of snow along their journey. The team's goal was for each team member to run every mile in less than 5 minutes. And, they all did just that! The team set the record to celebrate the centennial of their running club. They called their event "100 Miles for 100 Years."

● The relay team below must convert temperatures as they run. Follow the path that shows the correct conversions from Fahrenheit to Celsius temperatures. To convert the temperatures, follow the rule (°F - 32) ÷ 1.8 = °C.

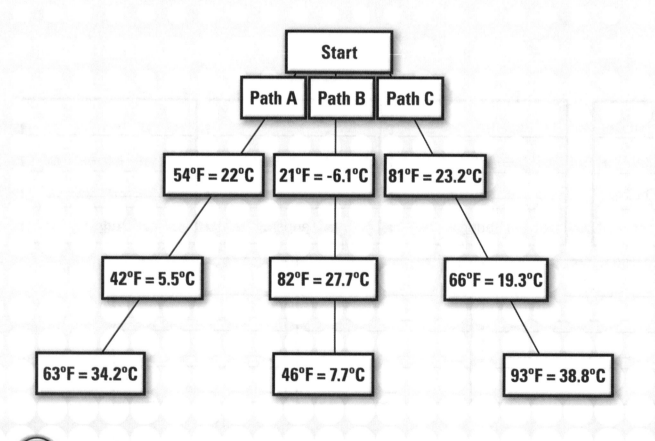

Start

Path A | Path B | Path C

54°F = 22°C | 21°F = -6.1°C | 81°F = 23.2°C

42°F = 5.5°C | 82°F = 27.7°C | 66°F = 19.3°C

63°F = 34.2°C | 46°F = 7.7°C | 93°F = 38.8°C

CD-104549

Beautiful Bender

Longest Time to Hold the Marinelli Bend Position
April 18, 2009

Iona Oyungerel Luvsandorj (Mongolia) is queen of the Marinelli bend. She can bend backward until her head is behind her shoulders and she is facing her ankles. At the same time, she supports her weight by a post that she clenches between her teeth! In 2009, Luvsandorj held this position for 50 seconds. To world-class contortionists, the Marinelli bend is simply one of the acts a flexible "bender" performs. This move is named after a nineteenth-century contortionist. The snake costume that Marinelli wore was so lifelike that it terrified the circus animals. Nothing is terrifying about Luvsandorj's move though. It's a perfect picture of grace and beauty.

● It appears as though Luvsandorj's body is split in two. Below are 10 words from the text that have also been split into two. But, unlike Luvsandorj's perfect pose, they have been put together incorrectly. The *first three letters* of each incorrect "word" really belong at the beginning of another incorrect "word" ending. Swap the first three letters of each "word" to put the words together correctly. Write the correctly spelled words on the lines.

1. ankce	
2. cleed	
3. fleelike	
4. graerneath	
5. lifght	
6. namition	
7. posles	
8. shonches	
9. undulders	
10. weixible	

Scuba Celebration

Most People Scuba Diving
August 17, 2009

If you are Indonesian, August 17 is your country's Independence Day. To celebrate Indonesia's 64th anniversary of its independence in 2009, the Indonesian Navy organized a special scuba diving event. On August 16, hundreds of people gathered at Malalayang Beach in Manado, Indonesia. They participated in a group scuba diving lesson. On the next day, Independence Day, both new divers and experienced divers made their way back to the beach. By the time they all dove into the water, a total of 2,486 participants were scuba diving. Then, a 31-minute ceremony took place once they all reached the ocean floor. The ceremony included raising the country's red-and-white striped flag—underwater!

- It is not a coincidence that diving was chosen as a way to celebrate this country's independence. Indonesia is an archipelago. It is made up of more than 17,000 islands lying between the Indian and the Pacific oceans. In Indonesia, you are never far from the water. "Our country is a strong maritime nation," said a government official. "It gives us pride [that we can prove it]."

Scuba diving is a wonderful way to tour the ocean. But, it requires equipment and training. The crossword puzzle on the next page contains scuba diving clues. Read the clues and complete the puzzle.

CD-104549

Across

1. You must have proper training before you _____ dive.

4. A scuba regulator _____ a mouthpiece allows you to breathe.

7. If you are _____ open foot fins, you will also need to wear dive boots.

9. Wear a weight belt to help keep you _____ the water.

10. _____ you buy your equipment, you might want to borrow or rent it first.

11. _____ dive alone!

13. You wear flappy fishy _____ on your feet.

15. Reef gloves will protect your _____ from getting scratched on the coral.

16. Dive gloves _____ your hands from the cold water.

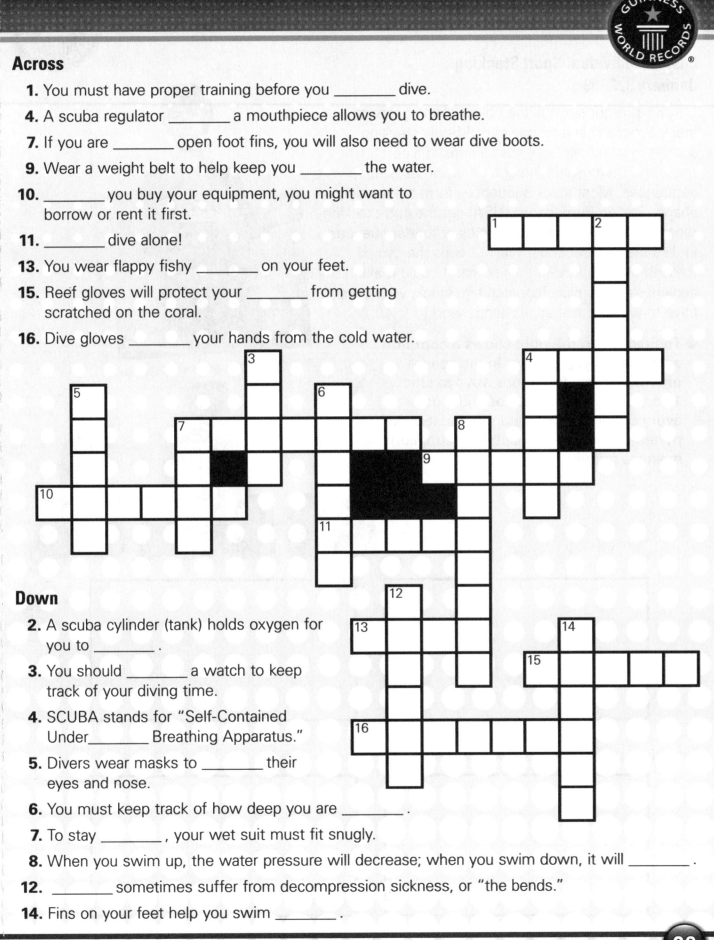

Down

2. A scuba cylinder (tank) holds oxygen for you to _____ .

3. You should _____ a watch to keep track of your diving time.

4. SCUBA stands for "Self-Contained Under_____ Breathing Apparatus."

5. Divers wear masks to _____ their eyes and nose.

6. You must keep track of how deep you are _____ .

7. To stay _____ , your wet suit must fit snugly.

8. When you swim up, the water pressure will decrease; when you swim down, it will _____ .

12. _____ sometimes suffer from decompression sickness, or "the bends."

14. Fins on your feet help you swim _____ .

Now You See It

Fastest Individual Sport Stacking
January 3, 2009

In what other sport is the object of the game to stack cups? What a unique sport! Sport stacking is a sport in which a player stacks cups in a certain order and then cycles through different stacking sequences. Most stack sequences form a pyramid shape. Steven Purugganan (USA) set the cup-stacking record by stacking cups in a series of four sequences in less than six seconds. With 12 cups, he cycled through the sequences so fast that it could make his audience's eyes blur. To watch him stack, your eyes have to work as fast as his hands work!

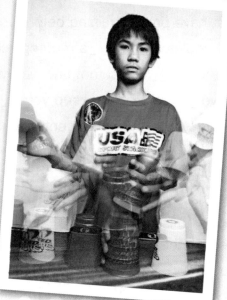

● The picture to the right shows a common way of stacking 12 cups. In the spaces provided, draw two more ways to stack 12 cups into pyramids. You must use every cup each time, and you must make pyramid formations. (Hint: One cup alone makes a pyramid shape.)

Now, find two ways to stack 10 cups.

Most Basketballs Spun Simultaneously on a Frame
May 25, 1999

World records are beaten often, and times are constantly being improved. But, no one has been able to beat Michael Kettman's (USA) record since 1999! Kettman spun 28 basketballs on a frame all at once. That's no easy feat. Kettman has appeared on numerous TV shows to demonstrate his basketball spinning. One challenge Kettman faces is that each ball has to spin long enough to get the other balls up and spinning also. Kettman gets the balls going first by spinning them on a metal post. Then, he transfers them to the frame that rests on his lap. To set the record, Kettman had to spin the last two balls on his fingertips! So far, no one else has been able to touch this record!

● When spinning 28 basketballs at once, the rule of the game is to be careful! The game below has a rule too. Try to figure out what the rule is by studying the numbers in the top section. Write the rule on the line. This will be an equation using a, b, and c. Then, use the rule to write the numbers for the bottom section.

c	20	34	30	68	29
a \ b	3 \ 2	4 \ 5	2 \ 8	6 \ 9	3 \ 5

Rule: _____

c	24	c	42	39	62
a \ b	5 \ b	6 \ 3	a \ 4	5 \ b	a \ 6

b = _____   c = _____   a = _____   b = _____   a = _____

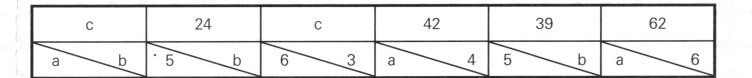

CD-104549

Cowgirl Kim

Largest Trick-Roping Loop by a Female
January 25, 2003

Are cowgirls real? You bet! Kimberly Mink (USA) is a cowgirl member of the Rhinestone Ropers, a Wild West road show. Mink and her family perform all sorts of traditional cowboy tricks—bullwhip cracking, gun spinning, trick shooting, knife throwing, and Mink's specialty, rope spinning. Simply spinning a rope loop isn't enough to get you into the record books, but Mink's spinning is special. In 2003, the rope loop she kept spinning around her body measured 76 feet 2 inches (23.21 m). That's plenty of rope to kink, twist, or trip on, but because Mink is a professional, none of those things happened.

● A list of rope-related words and a list of definitions appear below. Write the letter in the box beside the definition that you think matches the word best. If correct, the letters will spell, in order from top to bottom, the name of this Rhinestone Roper's trick horse.

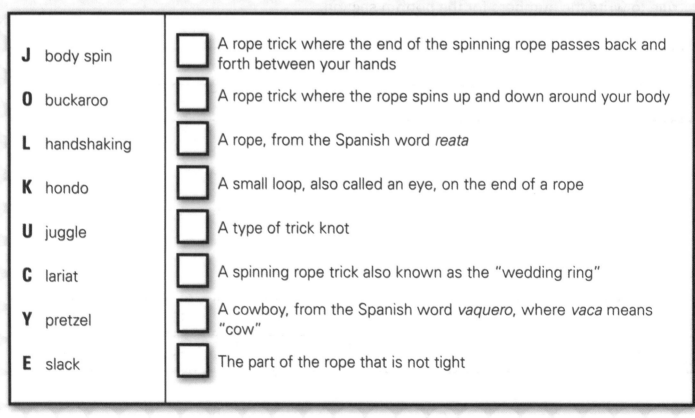

J body spin	☐	A rope trick where the end of the spinning rope passes back and forth between your hands
O buckaroo	☐	A rope trick where the rope spins up and down around your body
L handshaking	☐	A rope, from the Spanish word *reata*
K hondo	☐	A small loop, also called an eye, on the end of a rope
U juggle	☐	A type of trick knot
C lariat	☐	A spinning rope trick also known as the "wedding ring"
Y pretzel	☐	A cowboy, from the Spanish word *vaquero*, where *vaca* means "cow"
E slack	☐	The part of the rope that is not tight

CD-104549

A Skier from the Sky!

Oldest Heli-skier
July 9, 2008

Only daring young folks would be willing to ski down a giant ski slope that can only be reached by a helicopter, right? Well, don't be so sure. Christof Wieser (Austria) has been heli-skiing regularly for many years. His last journey made him the world's Oldest Heli-skier. He was 79 years, 8 months, and 20 days old at the time, just a couple of months shy of his 80th birthday. The remote location of the Austrian mountains makes them an ideal location for heli-skiers. Heli-skiers enjoy going to places so remote that they cannot be reached by ski lifts or trails. A helicopter ride is the only way to get to these locations for adventurous downhill skiing.

● Sometimes, a person's age can fool you. Use the clues to find out the age or birthday of each person in the puzzles below.

1. To get Madison's age, multiply Amira's age by 6. Madison's age is the numbers in Greg's age reversed, plus 14. Amira's age is a prime number that is less than 10 and greater than 6.

   Madison: _____

   Amira: _____

   Greg: _____

2. Jacob was born on the first day of the year. Cara was born 3 months, 14 days before Lisa. Lisa was born 8 months, 3 days after Jacob. What is Cara's birthday? _____

Answer Key

Page 6

13 + 8 = 21; 14 + 4 = 18; 21 + 3 = 24;
17 + 8 = 25; 27 + 9 = 36

Page 7

baby, 1; cat, 10; chair, 5; cow, 3;
hummingbird, 6; lake, 11; mouse, 12;
North America, 7; pony, 9; raisin, 8;
stool, 2; stream, 13; town, 4; worm, 14

Page 8

1. 494 + 37 = 531; 648 + 353 = 1,001;
2. 364 + 283 = 647; 187 + 57 = 244;
3. 624 + 549 = 1,173; 843 + 259 = 1,102

Page 9

1. 1 hour, 15 minutes; 2. 75 minutes;

Pages 10–11

X GAMES GOLD MEDALIST
amholdee athlete; eamholdee athlete;
eamsoldee atslete; eamsoldee etelsta;
eamsoldee etalste; eamesolde etalste;
eamesold eetalste; eamesold metalste;
eamesgold metalste; eeamesgold
metalst; eeamesgold medalst;
eeamesgold medalist; X gamesgold
medalist; X games gold medalist

Page 12

1. wisdom; 2. courage; 3. honesty;
4. kindness

Page 13

1. VI + III = IX or VII + III = X;
2. IX - V = IV; 3. V + II = VII

Page 14

battledore and shuttlecock

Page 15

In chart, from left to right: Carlos, Alvin;
Carlos, Jamie; Carlos, Jerry; Carlos, Kori;
Alvin, Jamie; Alvin, Jerry; Alvin, Kori;
Jamie, Jerry; Jamie, Kori; Kori, Jerry;
1. 10; 2. 7

Page 16

"Anything is possible. Nothing
is impossible."

Page 17

1. ball/hands/day; 2. try; 3. know/tricks;
4. part; 5. better/playing/game;
6. teach/kids; 7. seen/sorts; 8. love;
9. team/brothers; 10. change/smile

Page 18

Puzzle 1: Number of nollies: 6, 10, 16;
Seconds: 4, 8, 16, 24, 28, 36; Puzzle 2:
Number of nollies: 5; Seconds: 12, 18,
21. The rule is to multiply by 3 to get the
output or divide by 3 for the input.

Page 19

base; ball; play; team; cold; game;
help; snow

Page 20

491

Page 21

cube

Page 22

NAWATOBI
Answers will vary but may include:
FRIENDS: Pat and Emily, Jose, Aiden;
PLACES: New York, Mexico, Britain,
Russia; WEATHER: Snow and Hurricane,
Blizzard, Sunshine; VACATION: Fun
and Family, Eat Out, Disney; SPORTS:
Baseball, Hockey, Soccer, Tennis; FOOD:
Fruit and Hot Dogs, Burgers, French Fries;
BIRDS: Crows and Robins, Ostrich, Eagle;
FAMILY: Mom and Papa, Sister, Brother

Page 23

From first to last: Maggie, Jan, Leo,
Mario, Olivia

Page 24

Rachel, 39; Sean, 35; Gavin, 26; Owen, 15

Page 25

LUMBERJILL

Page 26

balance
rabbit; grasshopper; David
Weichenberger; frog; kangaroo

Page 27

Alexis; Hugo, 389 feet 7 inches; Graham,
389 feet 6 inches; Alexis, 468 feet
9 inches

Page 28

In chart: red, green, blue; red, green,
yellow; red, blue, yellow; green, yellow,
blue; 1. three; 2. three

Page 29

15; 30; 60; 120; 240; 480; 960; 1,920;
3,840

Pages 30–31

keepy uppy; kick; dribble; header;
perform; freestyle; bounce; practice;
champion; fancy

Page 32

Team A: 52 hours, 10 minutes; Team B:
50 hours, 22 minutes; Team C: 56 hours,
50 minutes; Team D: 53 hours, 7 minutes

Page 33

FLYIN' BRIAN

Page 34

202.67 miles

Page 35

Answers will vary but may include
buffalo/fox/human; Earth/planet/world;
day/month/year; football/soccer/tennis;
rake/shovel/wheelbarrow

Page 36

1. 723 × 5 = 3,615; 2,967 × 8 = 23,736;
2. 4,231 × 8 = 33,848;
6,508 × 3 = 19,524; 3. 6,913 × 6 = 41,478;
86,121 × 8 = 688,968

Page 37

scrummage

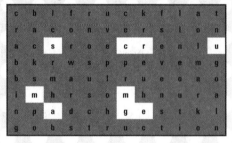

Page 38

The longest path is the left path (273.6
miles); (top path = 252; right path = 251.3;
bottom path = 249.3; left path = 273.6)

Page 39

sack race; shoe scramble; three-legged
race; obstacle course; wheelbarrow relay;
scavenger hunt; beanbag toss; water
balloon toss; tug-of-war

Pages 40–41

strike; big ears; goal posts; sour apple;
bicycle; pocket; snake eyes

Page 42

Alfonso: 31 feet 4 inches; Charlotte:
19 feet 11 inches; Lamar: 37 feet;
Terrance: 55 feet 6 inches

Page 43

Athens; angelfish; beetle; cheetah; giraffe;
greyhound; ostrich

Page 44

20, 28, 20

Page 45

WHEELZ; HELMET

Page 46

	1	2	3	4	5
1	J				N
2					
3			L	Mona	
4					
5		M			

Page 47

1. Ava, 40; Beth, 10; Claire, 4;
2. Simone, 9; Mom, 27: Grandpa, 72

Page 48

Rainbow Dave; events; win; Still; then; the; talented; was; hours; this; for; Stilts; spotting; She; tall; bright; pants; Around; when; again; race

Page 49

2/5	+	1/3	=	11/15
+				
3/10	+	1/2	=	4/5
=		+		
7/10		2/7		
		=		
1/7	+	11/14	=	13/14

Pages 50–51

1. (1,2) (4,3) (6,5) (4,3) (1,2); 2. (3,2) (6,1) (2,3) (1,1) (4,1) (3,4) (4,5) (4,3); 3. canoe; 4. life jacket

Page 52

$9 \times 9 = 81$; $7 \times 6 = 42$; $4 \times 9 = 36$; $6 \times 8 = 48$ or $8 \times 8 = 64$; $3 \times 9 = 27$

Page 53

pon-pon; jump; hop; bounce; leap; bound; spring

Page 54

1. recliner rugby; 2. desk diving; 3. nightstand netball; 4. mirror martial arts; 5. sofa sailing; 6. bookshelf bowling; 7. footstool fencing; 8. couch cricket; 9. love seat lacrosse; 10. hutch hockey

Page 55

The bottom layer should have 16 balls in the shape of a square (with four balls in the center). The second layer should have 9 balls (in 3 rows of 3). The third layer should have 4 balls, and the top layer should have 1 ball.

Page 56

ever 5. never; late 2. early; more 8. less; natural 1. fake; oldest 6. youngest; pulled 4. pushed; top 3. bottom; win 7. lose; wrong 9. right

Page 57

1. 2.9575; 2. 1.088; 3. 2.8613; 4. 3.9192; 5. 378.9; 6. 8.1477; 7. 38.213; 8. 3.736; HOP TO IT!

Page 58

hard; salt; speed; smaller; sand; tide; surfboard; over; carefully; knocked; water; sink

Page 59

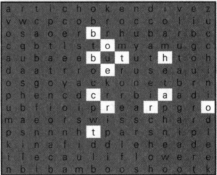

Pages 60–61

funambulist; Answers will vary but may include man; tight; flying; thin; strung; rims; with; for; slow; job; just; stop; path; hold; end; set; now; show; must.

Page 62

Colby, 468; Macon, 1,313.83; Leo, 71,120; Abe, 36,018

Page 63

Crack became interested in whips after seeing the movie *Indiana Jones and the Last Crusade.*

Page 64

B, D, C, A; (Volume of A is 15,444 in.², B is 8,060 in.², volume of C is 13,824 in.², and volume of D is 13,728 in.² .)

Page 65

LAND DIVE; 1. LAND; 2. LANE; 3. LINE; 4. LIVE; 5. DIVE

Page 66

The lines connect in this order: 36 feet 7 inches →73 feet 2 inches →146 feet 4 inches→292 feet 8 inches →585 feet 4 inches

Page 67

c

Page 68

sockball; magic; hopper; simple; potato

Page 69

top path = 263.2; right path = 230.7; bottom path = 188.3; left path = 220.8

Page 70

rise and shine dance

Page 71

WHAT A RALLY!

Page 72

"Ride Hard But Safe;" cross-country skiing; bobsleigh; speed skating; luge; ice hockey; Alpine skiing; curling; Nordic combined; snowboarding; ski jumping; freestyle skiing; skeleton; biathlon; figure skating; short track speed skating

Page 73

Second row from bottom: 11.54, 10.77, 12.17, 13.83; Third row from bottom: 22.31, 22.94, 26; Fourth row from bottom: 45.25, 48.94; top: 94.19

Page 74–75

Bob the Carrot

a	r	t	i	c	h	o	k	e	n	d	i	v	e	z
v	w	c	p	c	o	**b**	r	o	c	c	o	l	i	u
o	s	a	o	e	r	**h**	r	h	u	b	a	r	b	c
c	q	b	t	l	**o**	o	m	y	a	m	u	g	o	c
a	u	b	a	e	**b**	u	**t**	u	**h**	t	o	h	o	h
d	a	a	t	**r**	r	o	**e**	r	u	s	e	a	u	i
o	s	g	o	y	a	c	k	o	n	e	t	b	r	n
p	h	e	n	c	d	**c**	**r**	r	b	i	a	a	d	i
u	b	f	i	o	i	p	**r**	e	a	r	p	g	r	**o**
m	a	e	o	r	s	w	i	s	s	c	h	a	r	d
p	s	n	n	n	h	**t**	p	a	r	s	n	i	p	l
k	i	n	a	f	i	d	d	l	e	h	e	a	d	e
i	l	e	c	a	u	l	i	f	l	o	w	e	r	e
n	b	i	b	a	m	b	o	o	s	h	o	o	t	k

Page 76

Jaden: 69.90; Ebony: 35.74 miles; Dante: 30.48 miles

Page 77

7, 14, 21, 49, 77, 91, 98, 28, 70, 56, 42, 35, 84, 63

Page 78

camel; crane; ostrich; salamander; warthog; hedgehog; hippopotamus; parrot; penguin; butterfly; octopus; wallaby

Answer Key

Page 79

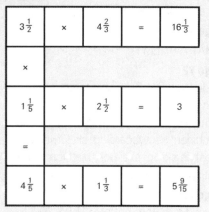

$3\frac{1}{2}$	×	$4\frac{2}{3}$	=	$16\frac{1}{3}$
×				
$1\frac{1}{5}$	×	$2\frac{1}{2}$	=	3
=				
$4\frac{1}{5}$	×	$1\frac{1}{3}$	=	$5\frac{9}{15}$

Page 80

FAMILY; everyone; come; flood; crossing; grab; monkey; cousin; lawyer; dinner; candy; door; break

Page 81

Answers will vary but may include 4-glad; 5-drain; 4-ding; 5-drool; 3-log; 5-brain; 5-brand; 2-go; 6-boring; 1-a; 1-I; 7-glaring; 8-groaning

Page 82

1. X + VI = XVI; 2. IX – V = IV;
3. XV – III = XII; 4. IV + XII = XVI

Page 83

SHRED; ranp/vert; lyPseop/McTwist; Ywxwhhanewh/Caballerial; jkhhea/nollie; dwhb lela/half-pipe; ckkbu bkkp/goofy foot; bwgea/fakie; ohwllu/slappy; jkoacnejz/nosegrind; khhea/ollie; pweh oheza/tail slide; bqjxkt/funbox

Page 84

36 ÷ 3 = 12; 54 ÷ 2 = 27; 93 ÷ 3 = 31; 60 ÷ 4 = 15; 64 ÷ 4 = 16

Page 85

grape; spine; flier; start; stare; white

Page 86

Path B

Page 87

ankles; clenched; flexible; grace; lifelike; named; position; shoulders; underneath; weight

Pages 88–89

Across 1. scuba; 4. with; 7. wearing; 9. under; 10. before; 11. never; 13. fins; 15. hands; 16. protect; **Down** 2. breathe; 3. wear; 4. water; 5. cover; 6. diving; 7. warm; 8. increase; 12. divers; 14. faster

Page 90

12-cup stacking: answers will vary but may include 6–6 and 10–1–1; 10-cup stacking: answers will vary but may include 6–3–1; 10

Page 91

The rule is a x b + 14 = c; bottom row: b = 2; c = 32; a = 7; b = 5; a = 8

Page 92

LUCKY JOE; L handshaking; U juggle; C lariat; K hondo; Y pretzel; J body spin; O buckaroo; E slack

Page 93

1. Madison, 42; Amira, 7; Greg, 82;
2. May 21